Mary & Ann Hogarth

from the old Frock-shop the corner of the Long Walk facing the Cloysters, Removed to y.ᵉ Kings Arms joyning to y.ᵉ Little Britain - gate near Long Walk Sells y.ᵉ best & most fashionable Ready Made Frocks, sutes of Fustian, Ticken & Holland, stript Dimmity & Flanel Wastcoats, blue & canvas Frocks & bluecoat Boys Dr.ᵃ, Likewise Fustians, Tickens, Hollands, white stript Dimitys, white & stript Flanels in y.ᵉ piece,

by Wholesale or Retale, at Reasonable Rates.

ALISON ADBURGHAM

SHOPPING IN STYLE

LONDON FROM THE RESTORATION
TO EDWARDIAN ELEGANCE

with 174 illustrations

By *the same author*

A PUNCH HISTORY OF MANNERS AND MODES, 1841–1940

SHOPS AND SHOPPING, 1800–1914

VIEW OF FASHION

WOMEN IN PRINT – WRITING WOMEN AND WOMEN'S MAGAZINES FROM THE RESTORATION TO THE ACCESSION OF VICTORIA

LIBERTY'S – A BIOGRAPHY OF A SHOP

Half-title: *Eighteenth-century shopping – the trade card of Mary and Ann Hogarth, sisters of William Hogarth who designed their card*, c. *1735*.

Title-page: *Edwardian Piccadilly – Swan & Edgar occupying the west side of the Circus in 1910, as it still does today, and claiming to be 'The leading West End Drapers'.*

Library of Congress Catalog card number 78-55198

Printed in Great Britain by
BAS Printers Limited, Over Wallop, Hampshire

CONTENTS

Oh, her lamps of a night! her rich goldsmiths,
print-shops, toy-shops, mercers, hardware-men,
pastry-cooks, St. Paul's Churchyard, the Strand,
Exeter Change, Charing Cross, with a man upon a
black horse! These are thy gods, O London!   CHARLES LAMB

Where has commerce such a mart,
So rich, so throng'd, so drain'd, and so supplied,
As London, opulent, enlarged, and still
Increasing London?   WILLIAM COWPER

A mighty maze! but not without a plan.   ALEXANDER POPE

*Early nineteenth-century City shops – gun flints, brushes, books and vegetables, all
for sale in Crooked Lane, c. 1840. Watercolour by G. Scharf.*

Foreword

THE skeleton of this book is topographical, outlining the growth of residential London from the Restoration, when the aristocratic owners of land began to restore and enhance their fortunes through speculative building. It is this growth that has dictated the pattern of shopping, and to follow it gives an understanding of the where, the why and the when of the siting of shops; and also, in a general sense, the who: who shopped where, and when.

More specifically, *who* was who? Anyone we *know*? Why yes, to be sure, many old friends . . . Mr and Mrs Pepys, James Boswell, Horace Walpole and Charles Lamb, Jane Austen, Robert Southey, Lords Nelson, Wellington and Byron, Thomas Creevey, Thackeray, Dickens, Augustus Sala, Mr and Mrs Carlyle and many more of slighter acquaintance. To come upon references to shops in their letters and other writings was exciting. They brought the topographical skeleton to life. And as the narrative came up to the close of the nineteenth century, it became possible to talk to people who had worked in shops in late Victorian and Edwardian times, such as the lady who had been employed in a hosiery department: 'It was all black stockings then,' she said, 'except white stockings for corpses. My grandmother had hers ready in a drawer.'

There were also customers with memories: 'I remember the Haymarket Stores, almost next door to Fribourg & Treyer's which is still there. It had a big square foyer with rails and hooks for tying up dogs, which were not allowed inside. It had a famous writing room which was always the rendezvous that my grandmother, great-aunt, uncle and mother used for meeting their friends in London.' And another: 'I remember that the assistants at Jay's were notorious for their regrettably light behaviour, and that the shopwalkers at Marshall & Snelgrove were the best dressed and the most gentlemanly, and those at Liberty's the most pertinacious.'

Such inconsequent memories give the flavour of a period more sharply than documented facts. And the snobberies and prejudices on both sides of the counter illuminate the shifting sands of class distinctions. Social history is from day to day, and it is the trivia of daily life, not the great events, that strike home.

To avoid intrusive footnotes, published books and other sources directly quoted are acknowledged in the text, with the details of publication in the list of references at the end of the book. This list also includes the sources I have found most rewarding with regard to the architectural development of London, the life of its residents and the history of its shops during the periods covered. I am grateful to the directors of many London firms who have given me access to their archives, and to Miss Margaret Swarbrick, archivist at the City of Westminster's Victoria Library, for her help. I would also like to thank Mr J. G. Links for his generosity in lending rare books from his own library, which have been most valuable both for information and illustration.

ALISON ADBURGHAM

Bishopsgate in the early eighteenth century: at centre a butcher prepares his meat on the pavement outside his shop.

Don Quixote, *the* Play of Sodom *and* Culpeper's Midwifery *are among the book auctioneer's wares in this engraving,* c. *1700.*

A Choice Collection of Books
being the Library of the late
famous Unborn Doctor, are
to be put to Sale this Day, and
to continue untill all be Sold.
at Mr. L——gs Auction in the
North West Corner of Middle
Moorfields. Catalogues may
be had at most of the eminent
Booksellers in the four Quarters
of Moorfeilds Gratis. the Books
may be Seen before or at the
time of Sale.

Sutton Nicholls excudit.

Come Sirs, and view this famous Library,
'Tis pity Learning shou'd discourag'd be:
Here's Bookes (that is, if they were but well Sold)
I will maintain't are worth their weight in Gold

**THE
COMPLEAT
AUCTIONER.**

Then bid apace, and break me out of hand:
Ne'er cry you don't the Subject understand:
For this I'll say - howe'er the Case may hit,
Whoever buys of me. - I teach 'em Wit.

1 Restoration London

Samuel Pepys and his London. Opposite: The City had been small enough to be fortified during the Civil War (above, in 1642–3) and is seen below from the Southwark bank of the Thames with London Bridge to the right. This crowded causeway, flanked with shops and dwelling houses, was London's only crossing of the river in Pepys's day.

A YOUNG MAN of twenty-two, with a Cambridge degree but no money, imprudently married the beautiful but portionless fifteen-year-old daughter of an exiled Huguenot. The diary which he began in 1660, four years after their marriage, gives an intimate insight into the day-to-day shopping of a young London couple at the time of the Restoration, the Great Fire and nine years thereafter. Embedded among events of national importance are the visits to his tailor and his wig-maker, to her favourite mercer and linen-draper. Here are the upholsterers and tradesmen who served them at home, the bookshops in which he loved to linger. Their taste in clothes and furnishings was above their income, and no great leap of the imagination is needed to enter into the anxieties of their daily disbursements. Samuel and Elizabeth Pepys are people we feel we know.

We can trace their increasing prosperity from the days when they were dependent on the patronage of a relative, through to the happy afternoon of 5 November 1668, spent 'going up and down among the coachmakers of Cow Lane . . . and at last did pitch on a little chariott, whose body was framed, but not covered, at the widow's, that made Mr Lowther's fine coach; and we are mightily pleased with it, it being light, and will be very genteel and sober.' The following month came the proud day when 'with my wife alone abroad, with our new horses, the beautifullest almost that ever I saw, and the first time they ever carried her, and me but once; but we are mighty proud of them. To her tailor's, and so to the 'Change, and laid out three or four pounds in lace, for her and me.'

Not all their shopping expeditions were so cordial, and tiffs about money were frequent. At the death of the Duke of Gloucester, national mourning being declared, 'I did give my wife £15 this morning to go to buy mourning things for her and me, which she did.' Then that evening, 'after I had looked over the things my wife had bought today, with which being not very well pleased, they costing too much, I went to bed in a discontent'. On another occasion Pepys had recorded having dined at home with Elizabeth and her sister-in-law: 'My wife snappish because I denied her money to lay out this afternoon; however, good friends again, and by coach set them down at the New Exchange, and I to the

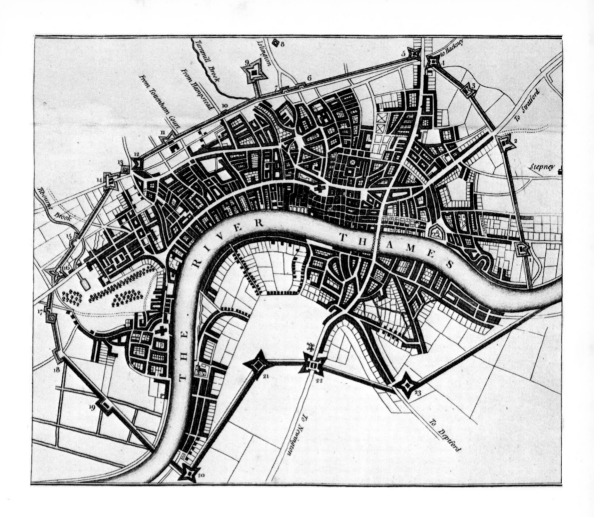

Exchequer.' Later the same day he himself did some important shopping: 'with Harman to my mercer's in Lombard Streete, and there agreed for our purple serge for my closett'.

To be fair to Samuel, he scolded himself for extravagance as much as his wife; but if it was a matter of clothes, he was able to argue with his conscience that it was necessary for him to dress well in his official position as Clerk of the Acts at the Navy Office: 'and so to Sir W. Turner's, and there bought my cloth, coloured, for a suit and cloake, to line with plush the cloakes, which will cost me money, but I find I must go handsomely, what ever it costs me, and the charge will be made up in the fruit it brings'. The Restoration was an immensely dressy period for men, and in order to 'go handsomely' it is clear he spent much more on clothes for himself than for his wife: 'So home to dinner, and thence by coach to the Old Exchange, and there cheapened some laces for my wife, and then to the great laceman in Cheapside, and bought one cost me £4, more by 20s than I intended, but when I came to see them I was resolved to buy one worth wearing with credit.' It was all right to haggle down the price of Elizabeth's lace at the Exchange, but there was no haggling with 'the great laceman in Cheapside', from whom he bought his own lace.

When they lived in Westminster, with his office in Whitehall, Pepys often wrote of going by coach to London. Neither Westminster nor Whitehall were in London. One drove through the village of Charing, along the Strand, and entered London at Temple Bar. The Strand was an ill-kept highway along which cattle were driven to Smithfield Market, and waggons carrying feeding stuffs, crops, vegetables and fruit from the surrounding farms and market-gardens rumbled through, jostling the coaches of the gentry. Lining the south side of the Strand were the walled gardens of noblemen's town mansions, in which they lived when attending Court and Parliament – the land at Westminster was too low-lying and marshy for large houses to be built there. Durham House, Arundel House, Salisbury House, Somerset House, Worcester House – all had their own stairs to the river, with their private craft to carry their lordships to Westminster or to Whitehall more pleasantly than through the hurly-burly of the Strand.

There was, of course, public river transport – the Thames was in effect the main link between Westminster and the City. From Parliament Stairs to London Bridge there were about thirty stairs where boats waited to take people along, or across, the river. For coaches, there were ferries with platforms. The river was almost as congested as the roads, with passenger boats knocked against by barges and commercial craft of all kinds. The chief hazard was passing under London Bridge, the widest arch of which was only thirty-six feet. At ebb tide the force of the water racing through these narrows created a cataract. Passengers for the Tower or Greenwich usually landed at the Three Cranes in Upper Thames Street, let the watermen 'shoot the bridge', and then embarked again at Billingsgate. An average of fifty watermen were drowned at the bridge every year.

Walking over the bridge was also dangerous, for it was scarcely twelve feet wide, and until Westminster Bridge was built in 1750 it was the only roadway to the southern counties. It carried all the waggons to and from the busy Southwark Market, to which many City dwellers walked to buy provisions, since prices were lower there than in the City markets. Each side of the bridge was lined by tall houses with shops on their ground floors, their backs projecting over the river and supported on great wooden beams. The medieval chapel of Thomas à Becket in the middle of the bridge was stripped at the Reformation and converted into a grocer's shop; and the original drawbridge became a butcher's shop. But most of the shops dealt in fashion goods. There were hatters, hosiers, haberdashers, milliners – everything for the would-be fashionable young man and for the girl on his arm.

Many of the streets in the City were no wider than London Bridge. It was said people could lean out of their overhanging upper windows and shake hands with their neighbours across the street. Sir William D'Avenant commented: 'Sure, your ancestors contrived your narrow streets in the days of wheelbarrows, before those greater engines, carts, were invented.' There was no stirring out in coaches, he said, because they were 'so uneasily hung, and so narrow as to look like sedans on wheels, and were subjected to the obstruction of waggons and carts, which were literally protected in their right of way by royal proclamations'. Paternoster Row was described in Strype's 1720 edition of Stow's *Survey of London*: 'This street, before the Fire of London, was taken up by eminent Mercers, Silkmen and Lacemen; and their shops were so resorted to by the nobility and gentry in their coaches, that ofttimes the street was so stop'd up that there was no passage for foot passengers.'

In contrast, Cheapside, traditional setting for all great civic occasions, was a handsome street lined by fine houses with ground-floor shops. In Elizabethan times, only the two richest retail traders, the goldsmiths and the silk mercers, had shops in Cheapside. In his *History and Survey of London*, published in 1756, W. Maitland writes of the distant past when 'it was beautiful to behold the glorious appearance of goldsmiths' shops in the South Row of Cheapside . . . four shops only of other trades in all that space'. By the seventeenth century more trades had edged their way in, but only the most prosperous retailers, linen-drapers and lacemen, could afford the high rents. It was still the most expensive shopping street in the City, and it seems inappropriate that tradesmen's wives should have sat at the doors of the shops to engage in badinage with men of fashion, enticing them in to buy. One must, however, take into account that the Restoration was a time of unprecedented socializing in the streets, the 'quality' mingling with work-people and joining in good-humoured back-chat. Class barriers had never before, and have never since, been less in evidence in open-air places of entertainment, such as fairs and public gardens, and there was the same kind of mingling in the shopping streets.

The shopkeeper's place of business was also his home, and as often as not he was the craftsman who made the things he sold – fanmaker, turner, jeweller, pewterer, basketmaker. He and his family lived at the back or over the shop, and the apprentices lived with them, their terms of apprenticeship including bed and board. Bed was often nothing more than a board, or straw mattress under the counter; but a good master took his responsibility *in loco parentis* for the lad's moral welfare just as seriously as his undertaking to teach him his trade. When the apprentice's indentures were completed, his master applied for him to be accepted as a member of his City Company, and that made him a Freeman. Apprentices were never girls, because it was not permitted for women to enter men's trades in the City, and shopkeeping was a man's trade. In any case, only Freemen of the City were allowed to practise a trade or open a shop within its boundaries. An exception was made for widows of Freemen to carry on their husbands' business, and of course many wives assisted their husbands during their lifetime. Again, a retailer who, in addition to his main shop, traded in one of the lock-up booths in the Royal Exchange, could allow his wife, or his daughter, to

Somerset House, one of the noblemen's mansions backing on the crowded thoroughfare of the Strand, all with access to the Thames and its relatively speedy means of transport.

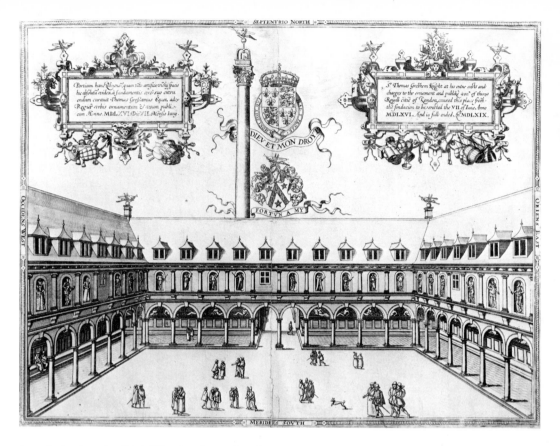

'man' the booth. Ned Ward, whose *London Spy* appeared in monthly parts from 1698, wrote that they 'sat in their pinafores, begging of custom with such amorous looks, and after so affable a manner, that I could not but fancy they had as much mind to dispose of themselves as the commodities they dealt in'.

The Royal Exchange was built in 1567 by Sir Thomas Gresham, merchant and mercer, at his own expense. The City Corporation gave him a site between Cornhill and Threadneedle Street, eighty houses having to be demolished. It was his patriotic ambition to create in London an international mercantile centre on the model of the one at Antwerp. Previously most mercantile business was conducted in the middle of Lombard Street, and sometimes in bad weather in the nave of St Paul's. The Royal Exchange contained an arcaded courtyard where traders grouped according to the country with which they had business. In the gallery above the arcades, there were some 160 small shops, little larger than booths and so dark that they had to be lit by candles even in the daytime. It was the rents for these shops, 40 shillings a year, that it was hoped would pay for the upkeep of the Exchange. The idea of lock-up shops without living quarters was quite new, and initially retailers showed no eagerness to rent them. But the Exchange was an immediate success in its main purpose as a meeting place for merchants; and in that time, before daily newspapers, it became *the* place in which to hear the

The Royal Exchange. 'Sr. Thomas Gresham Knight at his owne costs and charges to the ornament and publike use of this Royall citie of London, caused this place from the fondacion to be erected . . .'

latest political and foreign news. Fashionable gossipers soon began to use the Exchange as an elegant rendezvous, and retailers of fashion merchandise naturally followed them. Their shops dealt in some of the finest luxury goods in London, as well as spices and rarities from the East.

The favourite meeting places for men of learning and literature, on the other hand, were the bookshops. Indeed, they served almost as literary clubs. Customers were encouraged to sit down and read for as long as they liked at desks placed in the windows. The stock of new books was in unbound loose sheets, the binding being done to the order of each customer. Wealthy book-collectors liked to have all their books, as they acquired them, in uniform bindings. Often the title pages of new books were pinned up in the shop as advertisements, and contents pages were handed out as advance notices to likely buyers. Sometimes they were nailed up on the doorpost outside the shop to attract passers-by. Some booksellers allowed regular customers to borrow the sheets of a new work to take home and read 'on approval'.

The booksellers of the time were also the publishers. It was they who commissioned authors, or purchased their manuscripts; it was they who employed the printers or ran their own printing presses. This explains why there were so many bookshops in the City – in the Temple, Little Britain, Fleet Street, but most of all in St Paul's Churchyard. John Dunton, an enterprising publisher, idealist and eccentric bookseller, who published in 1693 the first women's periodical, *The Ladies' Mercury*, wrote in his autobiographical *Life and Errors* that by the time Queen Anne came to the throne in 1702 there were some 150 booksellers in London.

Since print runs of new books were small, secondhand copies were much sought after. Most bookshops did a secondhand trade, and book auctions were held in the Covent Garden piazza. There were stalls of secondhand books in many markets, and London booksellers visited the provincial markets and fairs, both to buy and to sell. The book section at Stourbridge Fair was internationally famous. Some booksellers started in the printing trade, turning out pamphlets, broadsides, political lampoons and the like; others started by selling secondhand books. John Dunton, when he opened his shop in the Poultry, built up his stock by the ingenious device of publishing just one book and, 'by exchanging it through the whole trade, it furnished my shop with all sorts of books saleable at that time'. Other booksellers started in a small way by importing books from the Continent. It seems that Pepys sometimes relaxed with a French novel (favourite diversion of his wife), although with a guilty conscience: 'Took physique all day, and, God forgive me, did spend it in reading of some little French romances.'

Westminster had its own enclave of booksellers and law stationers, whose stalls lined the walls of Westminster Hall itself, since the law courts then adjoined it. Some people thought it deplorable that this trade should be carried on in the nation's most magnificent and historic building; but more deplorable than the bookstalls were the booths of fashion merchandise and toys. A Mrs Mitchell had one booth, and there

Grawelot Del. & Mosley Inv.t et Sculp.

Westminster: 'The Dreadfull Hall by Rufus rais'd/For lofty Gothick arches prais'd' – but tainted by trade, with stalls of books, stationery, fashion goods and toys.

was Betty Lane, linen-seller and seamstress, from whom Pepys coaxed other favours than haberdashery. When the Great Fire was raging in the City, Pepys, 'being all in dirt from top to bottom', took a boat to Westminster thinking to get some clean clothes, 'but could not there find any place to buy a shirt or pair of gloves, Westminster Hall being full of people's goods, those in Westminster having removed all their goods'.

That the Westminster Hall traders were not just casual stallholders is shown by the fact that they allowed regular customers to run up accounts. On 14 July 1660, the day before Pepys moved house from Axe Yard, Westminster, to Seething Lane by the Tower, he noted in his diary, 'To Westminster Hall where I paid all my debts in order to my going away from hence.' Forty years later, when Ned Ward visited

17

Westminster Hall, the stalls were still there: 'We walked down by the sempstresses, who were very nicely fingering and pleating turnovers and ruffles for the young law students, and coaxing them with their amorous looks, obliging cant, and inviting gestures, to give so extravagant a price for what they might buy, that they may now and then afford to fling them a night's lodging into the bargain.'

Apart from groceries and bread, all foodstuffs were sold in the markets, and a distinction has to be drawn between shopping and marketing. Shopping was undertaken at leisure, a pleasurable activity. The shopper could dawdle over the choice of fashionable articles, over gloves and hosiery, lace and braiding, silks for her dresses, cloth for his suits, velvet for their cloaks. Even longer was likely to be taken over furnishings, table silver, and major household things, possibly involving several visits before a decision was arrived at or an order given. Rich merchants, whose houses in the congested City were too small for impressive furnishings, tended to spend their money on amassing gold and silver plate, unless they spent it building country houses or on charitable projects. Hence the great number of goldsmiths and silversmiths in the City.

In contrast, marketing was a daily activity undertaken by the servants of the household: choosing vegetables, fruit, meat and fish at the market stalls, paying cash, but haggling over prices and no doubt receiving commissions from the traders on large purchases. Vegetables were brought by waggon each morning from the farms that surrounded London; fish was brought up the Thames from fishing ports to Billingsgate. Large or small, the location of markets, the goods sold and the opening hours were all governed by City regulations. Different kinds of food had by law to be sold in specified market areas, in order that the quality could be inspected. A seller of bad meat might have it burned under his nose while he stood in the pillory. Bakers were often in court for selling undersized or poor quality loaves.

Gentlefolk, however modest their households, never themselves went shopping for food in the markets, a taboo that is illustrated by a little episode in Pepys's diary. It was a day when Samuel and Elizabeth had no maidservant to do the shopping – maidservants came and went rather rapidly in their household, especially if they were young and pretty. So Mr and Mrs Pepys did a little marketing together after dark, when there was small danger of being observed by any acquaintance. 'Thence to my wife, and calling at both Exchanges, buying stockings for her and myself, and also at Leadenhall, there she and I, it being candlelight, bought meat for tomorrow, having never a mayde to do it, and I myself bought, while my wife was gone to another shop, a leg of beef, a good one, for six pence, and my wife says it worth my money. So walked home with a woman carrying our things.' They did not so demean themselves as to carry their own meat home.

Leadenhall Market was the most important of London's markets, famous for meat all over England and even beyond. Charles II took the Spanish Ambassador, Don Petro de Rouquillo, to visit it, and the Ambassador is said to have commented, 'There's more meat sold daily in

OLD · LEADENHALL · MARKET

T. SULMAN del.

your market than in all the kingdom of Spain.' There were three squares, or courts: the first was the beef-market, the second a market for veal, mutton and lamb; and in the middle, and on the south and west sides, were houses and shops for fishmongers. At the east end was a market-house erected upon columns, with bell-tower and clock. In the passages leading out to the neighbouring streets, were fishmonger, poulterer and cheesemonger shops.

Leadenhall Market: although this drawing is of a much later date, the arrangement of shops and courts resembles that of Pepys's day.

It was at a baker's shop – the King's baker, no less – in Pudding Lane by Fish Street Hill that the Great Fire started on 2 September 1666. It raged from the Tower to the Temple, devastating the great commercial houses where wealthy merchants worked and lived with their families, and the tradesmen's shops which were also their homes. Few were able to salvage much of their stock or household goods. The booksellers suffered some of the most grievous losses and may also have contributed to the destruction of the cathedral, since they stacked as many books as they could in the crypt and against the walls of the choir. Pepys wrote on 25 September: 'Hear the great loss of books in St Paul's Churchyard, and at their Hall also, which they value at about £150,000, some booksellers being wholly undone, and among others, they say, my poor Kirton.' This was Joseph Kirton at the sign of the King's Arms – before street-numbering was introduced, shopkeepers identified their premises with hanging signs, the equivalent of inn signs. The following year Pepys wrote sadly, 'This day I hear Kirton, my bookseller, poor man, is dead, I believe of grief for his losses by the fire.'

When the City was rebuilt, it was not to St Paul's Churchyard that the booksellers returned, but to Paternoster Row. This street, that had been so famous for its fashion shops – mercers, lacemen, haberdashers, perfumers – was rebuilt 'with spacious shops, back warehouses, skylights and other conveniences made on purpose for their trade'. But most of the previous tenants had become established in neighbourhoods beyond the City, to the north and to the west, and had no wish to return, since their fashionable customers had also moved out of the City. So it was the booksellers, whose customers were not of the frivolous beau monde, who took over the spacious shops and warehouses, making Paternoster Row, together with Little Britain and Duck Lane behind, the centre of British bookselling and publishing. St Paul's Churchyard, their old stronghold, became the centre of Britain's wholesale drapery trade for the following two and a half centuries, until the next fire of London.

Tradesmen in fashion goods found temporary accommodation in Holborn, the Strand and Covent Garden. Pepys wrote on 26 September 1666: 'I away [from Whitehall] by coach home, taking up my wife and calling at Bennet's, our late mercer, who is come into Covent Garden to a fine house looking down upon the Exchange; and I perceive many Londoners every day come; and Mr Pierce hath let his wife's closett, and the little blind bed-chamber, and a garret to a silk man for £50 fine, and £30 per annum, and £40 per annum more for dieting the master and two prentices. So home, not agreeing for silk for a petticoat for her which she desired, but home to dinner and then back to Whitehall, leaving my wife by the way to buy her petticoat of Bennet.' Yes, she got her way before the end of the day – by what wheedling, we know not.

There was evidently profiteering by some people who had rooms to rent to refugees from the City; but those shopkeepers able to secure good premises found trade outside the City quite satisfactory. Pepys went with his wife 'to buy linen, £10 worth, for sheets etc. at the new shop over against the New Exchange'. The New Exchange was on the south side of the Strand. The owner of the shop 'is come out of London since the Fire, says his and other retail tradesmen's trade is so great here, and better than it was in London, that they believe that they shall not return nor the City be ever so great for retail as it was heretofore.' In this diary entry Pepys still refers to the City as London. The Strand was outside London.

The New Exchange was by no means new at this time. Designed by Inigo Jones, it was built in 1608 under the auspices of James I, who designated it Britain's Burse – a name that never caught on. It was a speculation of the Earl of Salisbury, the site being that of the stables of his riverside mansion, Durham House. Durham House stood where the Adam brothers in the next century built *their* speculation, the Adelphi. Lord Salisbury hoped to emulate the success of Sir Thomas Gresham's Royal Exchange, and the design was very similar: a two-storied classical building with a covered arcade at street level intended as a meeting place for merchants and businessmen. There were cellars beneath and a gallery above the arcades, which was lined with small shops. But the New Exchange proved to be too far from the City to serve its primary purpose, and the first floor was converted into private apartments, the ground floor arcades being given over to shopping booths.

Tenants of the booths had to comply with strict rules governing hours of business, cleanliness and comportment. A pair of stocks, provided for the detention of shoplifters, was an idea that modern retailers might like to copy. Trade was slow for a very long time, and, judging by Ben Jonson's *The Silent Woman* (Act I, Scene I), it seems to have been a place for chance encounters: 'He has a lodging in the Strand ... to watch when ladies are gone to the china houses, or to the Exchange that he may meet them by chance and give them presents.' At the time of the Great Fire many City shopkeepers were obliged to find accommodation in the New Exchange. One of these refugees was the bookseller Herringman, who set up his sign of the Blue Anchor in the street-floor arcade. He was the publisher of many important books, including Spratt's *History of the Royal Society*, which Pepys ordered in quires to have bound in similar binding to other books in his library. But it was not only scholarly interests that made Pepys a frequenter of Herringman at the Blue Anchor. He used the bookshop as a discreet place where Deb, dismissed from her place in the Pepys household, could leave notes telling him of her whereabouts. The New Exchange seems to have retained its rather clandestine character at least to the end of the seventeenth century when Ned Ward wrote of 'this seraglio of fair ladies ... the chiefest customers they had, I observed, were beaux who, I imagined, were paying double price for linen gloves or sword-knots, to the prettiest women, that they might go thence and boast among their brother fops what singular favours and great encouragement they had received.'

The contrasts of London before the Great Fire: many narrow streets with overhanging windows; London Bridge, the only 'road' to the south, too narrow to cope with its traffic (right); but also the grandeur of Cheapside (below right).

The shops and houses shown above, on the corner of Fleet Street and Chancery Lane, survived the Fire but were demolished in 1799 when Chancery Lane was widened.

ENTRÉE ROYALLE

MERE DV ROY TRES CHRESTIEN DANS LA VILLE DE LONDRES.

2 The first fashionable suburbs

COVENT GARDEN was London's first fashionable suburb, its development dating from 1630 when Inigo Jones designed a piazza for the 4th Earl of Bedford on land to the north of his recently rebuilt mansion in the Strand. This land, originally the garden of the Convent of Westminster, came into the possession of the Bedford family in 1552, and was already built over in a ramshackle way, housing an overflow of humanity from the City. The squeezing out of the poorest of the population into the various liberties beyond the walls created slum areas which were breeding grounds for epidemics of the plague. The Covent Garden development was much needed slum clearance.

Inigo Jones's plan was that of an Italian piazza, the south side formed by the garden wall of Bedford House, the north and east side formed by dwelling houses of noble proportions with coach houses behind. These houses were for 'persons of the greatest distinction', and at least three earls were amongst the first titled residents. The west side was reserved for a church, to be flanked on each side by a dwelling house. Once the piazza was completed, streets of more modest houses were planned to lead out of it. A licence was obtained for a vegetable market and for the fruit and flower stalls which, since the beginning of the century, had been allowed to trade in the shelter of the Bedford House garden wall. When the surrounding streets were built, many little shops came into being.

At the Restoration, when the Theatre Royal abutting on Drury Lane was re-opened, the whole neighbourhood gained a reputation for profligacy of the highest and lowest order, with taverns, lodging houses and brothels abounding. In the drama of the period, the piazza was often the setting for lovers' assignations, the scenario for stealthy intrigues. In Wycherley's *Love in a Wood, or St. James's Park*, Martha speaks of meeting Dapperwort 'in a piazza at midnight'; in Congreve's *Love for Love*, Mrs Flail, the lady of easy virtue, talks of taking a turn in a hackney-coach with a friend in Covent-garden Square. Drury Lane, although lined with noblemen's mansions, was a notorious beat of prostitutes, who traded by day and night. Pepys wrote on 21 March 1665: 'In our way the coach drove through a lane by Drury Lane, where abundance of loose women stood at the doors, which, God forgive me,

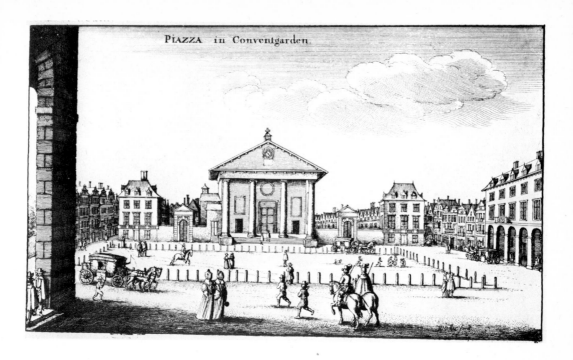

PIAZZA in Conventgarden.

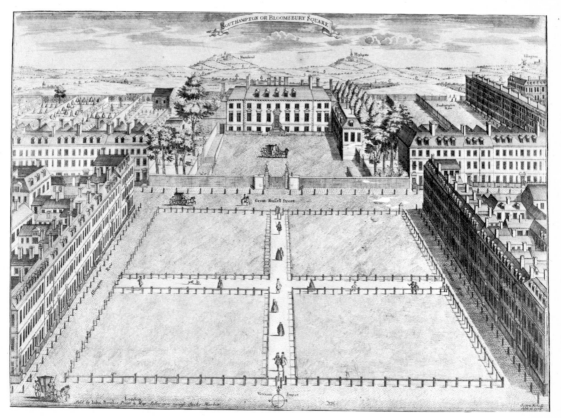

SOUTHAMPTON OR BLOOMSBURY SQUARE

25

Playing pell-mell.

did put evil thoughts in me, but proceeded no further, blessed be to God.' This was evidently quite early in the day, as he later drove home and then on to his office. Elizabeth's father lived in Long Acre and on another occasion Pepys wrote of 'setting her down by her father's in Long Acre, in so ill looked a place, among all the whore houses, that I was troubled at it, to see her go thither'. But Long Acre was celebrated for its coach-builders as well as its whore houses. In Long Acre, also, was Norris the picture framer – well positioned, since many artists lived in this quarter. Lely and Kneller, both court painters to Charles II, had their studios in the piazza. It was a quarter in which every layer of society was represented, from aristocrats down through literary and professional men, actors and journalists, tradesmen and craftsmen to the stallholders of the market and the riff-raff of the taverns and brothels.

Covent Garden was thus a microcosm of the new town life, suddenly set free at the Restoration from the constraints of the Commonwealth. Robert Bell wrote of this time in *Ainsworth's Magazine*:

The king himself set the example, and had scarcely finished the enthusiastic reception at Whitehall, when he retired in indecent haste and impetuous disorder, to lull his fluttered royalty in the lap of Mrs Palmer . . . and it became the custom, all at once, rising up out of the domestic lethargy of the Commonwealth, to live in public. . . . Everybody went abroad for enjoyment: and duchesses and citizens' wives, lords and scriveners, ladies of honour and sempstresses alike frequented those haunts of idleness and profligacy.

One piazza led to another. The 4th Earl of Southampton, who had demolished his town mansion at Holborn Bars and built a new Southampton House on his land in Bloomsbury, obtained in 1661 Letters Patent for a high-class development in the open fields in front of the mansion. The gardens of Southampton House made the north side of a square, the other three sides being enclosed by handsome houses that were quickly rented to rich city merchants. At first it was called Bloomsbury Piazza, but it soon became known as Bloomsbury Square. It was the first of all London squares, the prototype for a whole century of aristocratic residential developments. John Evelyn described it in February 1665 as 'a noble square, or piazza, a little town'. And like a little town it had a market, although not within the square. First called Southampton Market, then Bloomsbury Market, it was licenced for fish and flesh, and included a cake house to which Pepys took his wife and other ladies. New streets were made leading out of the square, lined with houses and small shops serving the neighbourhood. Bloomsbury never acquired the rakish reputation of Covent Garden. Dignified and quiet, the square itself was essentially residential.

St James's was the next fashionable development. The road leading directly north from St James's Palace had been a muddy track, described by John Evelyn as a quagmire. But in 1660 it was paved and named St James's Street. Charles II had chosen the great rambling palace of Whitehall to contain his Court, which employed some two thousand people, allotting the relatively miniature St James's Palace to his brother, James, Duke of York. James had a passion for the game of pell-mell, played along the road which became known as Pall Mall. Beyond the private gardens of the Palace, St James's Park became a fashionable quizzing ground by day and an adventure ground for less elegant dalliance by night – the gates were locked at 10 o'clock, but 6,500 people had keys issued by authority and nobody knew how many unauthorized keys were in use.

North of Pall Mall lay waste land owned by the Crown, and upon part of this the King granted a ground lease to Henry Jermyn, who had been Ambassador to France during the Civil War. He had served the Stuart family loyally in exile and at the Restoration was ennobled as Lord St Albans. In 1664 he obtained the warrant to build 'a square of thirteen or fourteen great and good houses'. But when first the Plague of 1665 and then the Great Fire accelerated the migration from the City, he revised his plan. The great and good houses standing in their own gardens – houses for aristocrats – might have proved difficult to rent, since aristocrats liked to own the land their houses stood on; whereas twenty-two houses, still good but not quite so great, would more easily be rented to wealthy City merchants. The houses were linked in uniform terraces with a common garden in the centre. At first styled 'the Piazza', it soon became known as St James's Square.

Around this rich men's enclave were planned the neighbourhood necessities of a church (St James's, built by Wren), streets of shops and modest houses for professional people (King Street, Charles Street, Jermyn Street) and, of course, a market. This was laid out on a site close to where Piccadilly Circus now is. At first called St Alban's Market, then St James's Market, it was described by Strype as 'a large place with a commodious Market House in the midst, filled with Butchers' shambles, besides the stalls in the Market-place for country Butchers, Higglers, and the like; being a market now grown to great account, and much resorted unto, as being well served with good provisions'.

Piccadilly was at this time named Portugal Street for most of its length as a gesture to Charles's queen, Catherine of Braganza. Only a 280-yard stretch from the top of the Haymarket was called Piccadilly. The origin of the name is not wholly certain, though the best-documented account is given by C. L. Kingsford in his *Early History of Piccadilly*. He associates it with a tailor named Robert Baker who bought, some time before 1612, about one-and-a-half acres of land at the Windmill, north of the Haymarket, and built himself an imposing house. This property was popularly nicknamed Pickadilly Hall, Baker's fortune being said to have been made by the sale of pickadills, which were stiff supports worn under the ruffs that were fashionable at the time he was in business. At his death in 1624, Pickadilly Hall was documented as 'divers houses and messuages', and soon the name was loosely applied to the whole locality from Coventry Street to Portugal Street.

Portugal Street, leading to Hyde Park Corner toll-gate, was the highway to Reading and the west, and was deeply rutted by the cumbersome six or twelve-horse coaches that had come into use during the Commonwealth. There were plenty of taverns along it, but no big houses until 1664 when Lord Clarendon, the Lord Chancellor, built a

A pickadill: in detail and in action as a support beneath a ruff.

mansion with an elegantly urban view looking straight down St James's Street to the Palace. To the north, it had a sweetly sylvan prospect over fields to the heights of Hampstead. Alas for Lord Clarendon, all too soon after he had moved into his enviably placed residence, he had to flee the country to escape impeachment for high treason. His house was bought by the Duke of Albemarle, who renamed it Albemarle House – only to re-sell it within a few years to a syndicate headed by John Hinde, a goldsmith-banker, who pulled it down within twenty years of its erection and developed the site as a residential estate. Thus Albemarle Street, Dover Street and Bond Street came into being – Bond Street taking its name from Sir Thomas Bond, Controller of the Household of the Queen Mother Henrietta Maria, a member of John Hinde's syndicate. At that time, 1686, it consisted of only the two hundred yards or so that were later named Old Bond Street when the street was extended northwards as New Bond Street – a desultory process, lasting from 1700 to 1730.

Another great house on Portugal Street was that built for Lord Berkeley of Stratton two years after Clarendon House. When he died in 1678, his widow asked John Evelyn to advise her; and on 12 June 1684 he noted in his diary:

I went to advise and give direction about the building two streetes in Berkeley Gardens, reserving the house and as much of the garden as the breadth of the house. In the meantime I could not but deplore that sweete place should be so much straiten'd and turned into tenements. But that magnificent pile and gardens contiguous to it, built by the late Lord Chancellor Clarendon, being all demolish'd, and designed for piazzas and buildings, was some excuse for my Lady Berkeley's resolution of letting out her ground also for so excessive a price as was offered advancing neere £1000 per annum in mere ground-rents; to such a mad intemperance was the age come of building about a citty, by far too disproportionate already to the nation; I having in my time seen it almost as large again as it was within my memory.

Two new streets came into being from the garden of Berkeley House: Stratton Street and Berkeley Street. And the houses that flanked them were hardly 'tenements' in the modern sense. They were the beginning of the aristocratic district which later became known as Mayfair.

The name Mayfair came from a cattle fair held on waste land to the north of Portugal Street. Letters patent were granted in 1686 and 1688 to hold a fourteen-day market for live cattle on 1 May every year on Brookfield, near Hyde Park Corner toll-gate, which was then a rural crossroads with a few taverns for the drovers who brought their beasts to town. Livestock on the hoof had to be taken over from the country drovers at this point and escorted to Smithfield by drovers employed by the City Corporation, who were distinguished by brass armbands. The cattle fair soon developed into a general jollification with tents and booths, hucksters, freaks, fortune-tellers, all the fun of the fair. The fun increased every year until the riff-raff had virtually taken over from the cattle. The authorities declared the fair to be 'one of the most pestilent nurseries of impurity and vice . . . the stalls and booths were not for trade but for musick, shows, drinking, gaming, raffling, lotteries, stage plays and drolls.' The side-shows were then forbidden by royal proclamation. After Queen Anne's death in 1714 the incitements to impurity and vice began to return; but to a more restricted area, since Edward Shepherd, a property developer who leased the land from Sir Nathanial Curzon, had started building a permanent market-place centred on a two-storey market-house. The ground floor consisted of aisles for butchers' shops, and around the external boundaries there were other shops 'connected with culinary purposes'. The second storey was used as a theatre at the time of the May fair.

A whole neighbourhood gradually grew round this market square, with permanent shops for domestic goods. Such houses as were not shops were modest little dwellings for skilled craftsmen and artisans. There was somebody who could sell you anything you might need from day to day, or who could undertake any kind of repair work you might require. Shepherd Market had grown into a little village with its own independent life. And as Mayfair's little village it is still regarded, with its village shops – perhaps the most unchanged place in all central London.

With the most aristocratic residents of the City moving westwards, it was natural that the most ambitious City shopkeepers should follow them. Robert Davis, a hatter of Bishopsgate, became leaseholder from the Crown of five houses in St James's Street in 1676. He set up his shop in one, and rented the others. Ten years later, another emigrant from the City bought the lease of seven houses on the site where a tennis court had formerly stood by the north-east corner of St James's Palace. This was George James Lock, a successful Turkey merchant – that is, an importer of coffee. Like Davis, he lived in one of the houses and rented the other six. One was taken by George Seddon, a well-known clockmaker. The largest was taken by a Mr Lodge for a chocolate house. When chocolate

Early eighteenth-century pleasures: lively goings-on at the May fair and a spirited debate at the coffee house.

was introduced into England, Parkinson's *Herbal* (1640) denounced it as
'a drink that might do well enough for natives, but for Christian tastes it
must be reckoned as nothing more or less than a wash for hogs'. But by
the end of the century King William enjoyed a cup of 'jockolate', and by
the middle of the eighteenth century the once despised hogwash was
considered an elegant drink. With coffee and tea, it was bought in
considerable quantities by the Duke of Bedford's household from
Tom's Coffee House in Covent Garden. One must suppose that Mr
Lodge of St James's also served coffee, and was a useful customer for Mr
Lock's imports. Many Turkey merchants opened their own coffee
houses as outlets for their importing activities.

The earliest record of coffee being sold in an English shop was in
Oxford in 1648, and the first London coffee shop was opened in the City
by a Turk four years later. His customers were invited to drink coffee on
the premises, or to buy berries to take home. Soon many coffee shops
were opening, selling also cocoa-berries from the West Indies and the
vastly expensive dried leaves of the tea plant from China. Most of these
shops served bowls of coffee or chocolate to drink on the premises. Until
the Court moved to St James's after fire destroyed Whitehall Palace in
1697, there were only two coffee houses in the St James's quarter: White's
(1693) and Ozinda's (1694). But a new clientele was created by the
presence of the Court in the neighbourhood, and the Cocoa Tree opened

George
William **Brummell** Esqr

Beau Brummell was often weighed on the Great Scales of Berry Bros. & Rudd, and each time it was recorded whether he was wearing half-boots, boots, or boots and great-coat, thereby affecting his weight (left). The custom continued into the twentieth century, as Frank Dadd's painting of 1911 indicates (right).

in 1698. Four years later, the Smyrna Coffee House, a favourite with Dean Swift and Matthew Prior, was established in Pall Mall by a Turkey merchant whose imports included tobacco as well as coffee; and within another three years the Thatched House Tavern had opened in St James's. The century of coffee houses and of conversation had begun.

Coffee houses were masculine strongholds, the predecessors of gentlemen's clubs, so it was natural that St James's shops should cater for the requirements of fashionable gentlemen. The shop of Davis the hatter was only a few doors away from the St James's coffee house, a meeting place of Whigs; and the names on Davis's earliest surviving order books are those of the great Whig families: Marlborough, Bedford, Devonshire, Walpole. Jermyn Street became noted for its shirtmakers – still is – and had the most elegant haberdashers, barbers, perruquiers, the most highly esteemed tobacconists. St James's Street itself was noted for its gunsmiths, hatters and bootmakers.

Nevertheless, there were two notable women shopkeepers. In 1696 Widow Bourne opened a grocer's shop at the sign of the Coffee Mill, No. 3 St James's Street, thus establishing the business which after two changes of ownership became Berry Bros. & Rudd, wine merchants, who are still there. Their cellars run out for 150 feet to the centre of St James's Street. From 1765, this shop offered its aristocratic customers an unique service: they could be weighed on the Great Scales used for weighing tea, sugar and spices. A series of books kept through the years registered the weights of 'people of fascination' (Henry Fielding's phrase), and included six generations of the royal families of England and France. To have one's name entered was a confirmation of social status, and some patrons were regularly weighed from young manhood to ripe old age. The Great Scales are still in the unaltered shop.

The other woman shopkeeper was Mrs Elizabeth Neale, who ran a fruit shop. Everyone called her Betty, including Horace Walpole, who in a letter to George Montague on 23 June 1750 wrote: 'I had a card from Lady Caroline Petersham to go with her to Vauxhall. . . . She had brought Betty, the fruit-girl, with hampers of strawberries and cherries from Rogers's and made her wait upon us, and then made her sup by us at a little table.' Betty retired when comparatively young, and at her death received the posthumous distinction of an obituary in the *Gentleman's Magazine*, 30 August 1797:

Died age 67, at her house, facing St James's Street, at the top of Park Place, Mrs Elizabeth Neale, better known by the name of Betty. She had kept, for very many years, a house in St James's Street as a fruit shop, from which she had retired about fourteen years. She had first pre-eminence in her occupation, and might justly be called the Queen of Apple-women. Her knowledge of families and characters of the last and present age was wonderful. She was a woman of pleasing manners and conversation, and abounding with anecdote and entertainment. She was born in the same street in which she ever lived.

There is no suggestion that the Queen of Apple-women employed her charms to the same ends as the Princess of Orange-sellers, Nell Gwyn.

It was in St James's Market that William Fortnum met Hugh Mason, who was one of the market shopkeepers. Fortnum was a young man from Oxfordshire seeking work. He took lodgings with Mason and got a position as a footman in the household of Queen Anne. One of the footmen's duties was to refill the royal candlesticks each night, since royal candles were never lit twice; and it was their legitimate perk to sell the partly used candles to the ladies of the household. By saving the proceeds of this fringe benefit, Fortnum was able to retire in 1707, when still quite young, and set up a grocer's shop with Hugh Mason. Their little shop was in Jermyn Street, the site being on part of the land covered by Fortnum & Mason's present building. With his Palace connections, Fortnum was able to secure grocery orders from the Royal Household, which in turn automatically brought him the custom of most aristocratic households. Since all the houses of the neighbourhood did not have their own stables, Hugh Mason realized that a livery stable providing space for private carriages would be a lucrative investment. Daytime stabling was also needed for the pack horses and dray horses bringing in goods from the country. So he built stables at the rear of the shop, giving the mews his own name: Mason's Yard. Mason's Yard is still there, a turning off Duke Street St James's. The Palace connection was kept up by William Fortnum's son; and his grandson, Charles Fortnum, entered Queen Charlotte's service. Charles retired in 1788 to give all his time to the family shop. But it seems he could not resist the

glamour of Court life, since in 1807 he returned to be Page of the Presence, the equivalent of today's Equerry or Private Secretary.

In 1747 a grandson of George James Lock, the Turkey merchant who had come to Pall Mall in 1686, was apprenticed to Charles Davis, son of the hatter Robert Davis, who moved to St James's Street from the City ten years earlier. During the customary term of seven years, to be completed on the apprentice's twenty-third birthday, he lived as one of the family; and like quite a few apprentices, when the master had no son to inherit his business, James Lock married his master's daughter a few years after he had completed his indentures. When Charles Davis died in 1759, the young couple took over No. 6 St James's Street, and the facia board thereafter bore the name LOCK, as it does today. Lock's was by no means without near rivals. Since at least 1730 a hatter and hosier named Yeow had had his shop on the corner of Bond Street and Piccadilly. In 1779 a Mr Dolman, hatter and hosier, came to No. 8 St James's Street, the house where Lord Byron was lodging when in 1812 he became famous overnight with the publication of *Childe Harold*. At No. 79 there was a firm of hatters named Money & Davis; and in 1807 yet another hatter, James Swallow, opened at No. 2, next door to Berry's the wine merchants and grocers.

In 1783 a duty on hats was imposed by William Pitt the Younger. All hatters were required to render the tax to the Government. The hatters, of course, required all customers to render it to them in the first place.

Paper stamps, receipts for the tax, had to be fixed inside hats at the time of sale. A newspaper cutting dated 1787, in the Finsbury Local History Collection, reported: 'Sunday evening a man was detected in Northampton Chapel, in the Spa-fields, in the act of stealing the stamps out of the hats of several of the congregation. Three-and-twenty stamps for hats, all of which had been evidently used, were found on him. He was secured in New Prison.' Let it not be thought this gentleman was in business with any of the aristocratic hatters of St James's! The law was amended in 1796 to substitute for the paper ticket a durable stamp on the hat lining. Later, Pitt imposed a Powder Tax which put wigs out of fashion – and also cocked hats, since they were designed to complement the wig. They were replaced for 'people of fascination' by the tall silk hat, although there were conspicuous adherents to the more romantic cocked hat. Lord Nelson, of course, was one. In 1794, Lock's designed a fitted eyeshade to his usual cocked hat to cover the eye blinded at the Siege of Calvi; and he ordered a similar model before sailing from Portsmouth in 1805 on the voyage that culminated in the battle of Trafalgar. The hat is on his tomb in Westminster Abbey. Not to be outhatted by Nelson, the Duke of Wellington wore a Lock cocked hat, splendidly plumed, at the battle of Waterloo. Wellington's boots were made by the royal bootmaker Hoby, whose shop was on the corner of St James's Street and Piccadilly. According to Captain Gronow's *Reminiscences and Recollections*, 'Hoby was the first man to drive about London in a tilbury . . . painted black and drawn by a beautiful black cob. He was so great a man in his own estimation that he was apt to take rather an insolent tone with his customers. He was, however, tolerated as a sort of privileged person . . . and he died worth a hundred and twenty thousand pounds.'

Aristocratic St James's Street, looking south to the Palace.

Lock of St James's Street, their premises unaltered since the eighteenth century.
Left: *Lock's woven-silk hat label.*

Benjamin Cole.

at the Sun in St. Pauls-Church-Yard

LONDON.

Imports & Sells all sorts of Cambricks,
Lawn, Macklin & English Lace, & Edgin,
Where all Merchants, Dealers &
Others may be Furnish'd, Wholesale or
Retail at Reasonable Rates.

Shopping life in the rebuilt City. Left: *A flourishing pawnbroker and silversmith in Grace Church Street ('Lends Money on Plate, Watches, Jewells, Wearing Apparel, Household Goods') and (far left) Benjamin Cole of St Paul's Church-Yard.* Above: *In Cheapside c. 1750, when hanging shop signs were still much in evidence, their removal not being enforced until 1762.*

3 The rebuilt city

AT THE TIME of the Great Fire Holborn was one of the streets where City tradesmen found temporary accommodation. Some returned to the City when it was rebuilt, others acquired permanent premises; and the presence of well-known City tradesmen in Holborn attracted other shopkeepers. It was an excellent situation. The fine houses of Lincoln's Inn had been completed in Charles I's reign, and Clare Market had been set up in Lincoln's Inn Fields at the end of the Commonwealth. Lord Southampton's Bloomsbury Square was also nearby, while the building of Red Lion Square in 1684 brought still more rich residents to the neighbourhood.

Nevertheless, the rebuilt City, with a new Royal Exchange risen out of the ashes of the old, reasserted its supremacy over Holborn, Covent Garden and the Strand as the undisputed locality for all the best silk mercers, woollen and linen merchants, lacemen, goldsmiths and jewellers. The City was still where the money was made, and still where much money was spent. Moreover, the average wealth of the resident population, in spite of the fashionable exeunt, was higher than before. For the movement to the west was balanced by a movement to the east by the poorest citizens who had no homes to return to after the fire and the subsequent clearance of the more squalid city tenements that had not been burned down. Just as the 'West End' had come into being, so had the 'East End' – with the City of London between.

Most of the streets were a little wider than before. The houses, in brick instead of wood, no longer had their upper storeys overhanging, and fewer shop signs jutted out above the pavements. The old shop and tavern signs were great heavy things of copper, pewter, or wood, painted and gilded, and there had been cases of them crashing down and killing passers-by. Where shops had been rebuilt after the Fire, the hanging signs had mostly been replaced by carved shop signs on stone panels let into the face of the building. The numbering of houses as a means of identification, instead of signs, is believed to have begun in Great Prescott Street in 1708; but the removal of all hanging signs was not enforced until 1762. Even so, some contrived to remain in Wood Street and Whitecross Street until 1773.

The merchants were at the top of the City hierarchy. Daniel Defoe,

The City 'Prentice at his Masters door.

himself the son of a butcher, made clear in his *The Complete English Tradesman* (1726) the distinction between tradesmen and merchants: 'In England, the word merchant is understood of none but such as carry on foreign correspondence, importing the goods and growth of other countries, and exporting the growth and manufactures of England to other countries. These in England, and these only, are called merchants, by way of honourable distinction.' Tradesmen ranked lower in the social scale. Nevertheless, they had to be Freemen of the City of London in order to trade there, and

may on occasion keep company with gentlemen as well as other people; nor is a trading man, if he is a man of sense, unsuitable or unprofitable for a gentleman to converse with, as occasion requires; and you will often find, that not private gentlemen only, but even ministers of state, privy-councillors, members of parliament, and persons of all ranks in the government, find it for their purpose to converse with tradesmen, and are not ashamed to acknowledge, that a tradesman is sometimes qualified to inform them in the most difficult and intricate, as well as the most urgent affairs of government; and this has been the reason why so many tradesmen have been advanced to honours and dignities above their ordinary rank, as Sir Charles Duncombe, a goldsmith; Sir Henry Furness, who was originally a retail hosier; Sir Charles Cook late one of the Board of Trade, a merchant; Sir Josiah Child, originally a very mean tradesman . . . but whose posterity by his two daughters are now Dukes of Beaufort and of Bedford, and his grandson Lord Viscount Castlemaine.

While daughters of impoverished aristocrats were

so stiff upon the point of honour, that they refuse to marry tradesmen, nay, even merchants, though vastly above them in wealth and fortune . . . the gentlemen of quality act, I may say, with much more judgement, seeing nothing is more frequent than when any noble family are loaded with titles and honours rather than fortune, they come down into the City, and choose wives among the merchants and tradesmen's daughters to raise their families; and I am mistaken, if at this time we have not several duchesses, countesses, and ladies of rank who are the daughters of citizens and tradesmen.

Later, in Regency times, City heiresses who propped up the possessions of great landed families were nicknamed 'golden dollies'.

Defoe gave many warnings to young tradesmen against apeing their betters in luxurious living:

This is an age of gallantry and gaiety, and never was the City transposed to the Court as it is now; the play-houses and balls are now filled with citizens and young tradesmen, instead of gentlemen and families of distinction; the shop-keepers wear a different garb now, and are seen with their long wigs and swords, rather than with aprons on. But what is the difference in the consequences . . . jails filled with insolvent debtors . . . commissions of bankruptcy every week in the Gazette. . . . It is an age of drunkenness and extravagance, and thousands ruin themselves by that; it is an age of luxurious and expensive living, and thousands more undo themselves by that; but, among all our vices, nothing ruins a tradesman so effectually as the neglect of his business. . . . Very ordinary tradesmen in London keep at least two maids, and some more, and some a footman or two besides.

Twenty years later, R. Campbell in his *The London Tradesman*, although writing that the mercer 'must dress neatly, and affect a Court Air, however far distant he may live from St James's', also warned against extravagant living:

Measuring and fitting at a tailor's shop in the first half of the eighteenth century.

The Business of a Mercer requires a very considerable Stock; Ten Thousand Pounds, without a great deal of prudent Management, makes but a small Figure in their Way; nor will the Profits, though reasonable, admit of the Expense of a Nobleman: A City and Country House, a Pack of Hounds in the Country, and a Doxy in a Corner of the Town, Coaches, Horses, Gaming, and the polite Vices of St James's, cannot be afforded out of the Profits of Silk and Velvet.

Of the 'Gold and Silver Lace-man', Campbell wrote:

He ought to speak fluently, though not elegantly, to entertain the Ladies; and to be Master of a handsome Bow and Cringe; should be able to hand a Lady to and from her Coach politely, without being seized with the Palpitation of the Heart at the Touch of a delicate Hand, a well-turned and much exposed Limb, or a handsome Face: But, above all, he must have Confidence to refuse his Goods in a handsome Manner to the extravagant Beau who never pays, and Patience as well as Stock to bear the Delays of the sharping Peer, who pays but seldom.

Peers were particularly hazardous customers, since they were in the happy position of enjoying immunity from arrest for debt.

Campbell wrote very fully of the delicacies required of a stay-maker. Stay-makers were always men 'because the Work is too hard for Women, it requires more strength than they are capable of to raise Walls of Defence about a Lady's Shape'. The stay-maker

ought to be a very polite Tradesman . . . and possessed of a tolerable Share of Assurance and Command of Temper to approach their delicate Persons in fitting on their Stays, without being moved or put out of Countenance. He is obliged to inviolable Secrecy in many Instances, where he is obliged by Art to mend a crooked Shape, to bolster up a fallen Hip, or distorted Shoulder . . . to him she reveals all her natural Deformity, which she industriously conceals from the fond Lord, who was caught by her slender Waist.

When Dr Johnson first came to London, he lodged with a stay-maker in Exeter Street – one wonders whether he wheedled any secrets from this Mr Morris about the shape of his clients.

Defoe's description of shopkeepers' *folies de grandeur* is paralleled by Mrs Mary Manley's description of shop assistants in the *Female Tatler* of 1709. She wrote of the shops of Ludgate Hill as

Above: Documentary evidence of the stay-maker's need to be 'a very polite Tradesman'; the corset is in two parts, laced front and back, and is being fitted over the lady's chemise.

perfect gilded Theatres, the variety of wrought Silks so many Changes of fine Scenes, and the Mercers are the Performers in the Opera. . . . They are the sweetest, fairest, nicest, dished-out Creatures; and, by their elegant Address and soft Speeches, you would guess them to be Italians. As People glance within their Doors, they salute them with – 'Garden-silks, Ladies, Italian Silks, Brocades, Tissues, Cloth of silver, or Cloth of gold, very fine Mantua Silks, Geneva Velvet, English Velvet, Velvet embossed.' We went into a Shop which had three Partners: two of them were to flourish out their Silks; and, after an obliging Smile and a pretty Mouth made, Cicero like, to expatiate on their Goodness; and the other's sole Business was to be Gentleman Usher of the shop, to stand completely dressed at the Door, bow to all the Coaches that pass by, and hand Ladies out and in. We saw Abundance of gay Fancies, fit for Sea-captains' Wives, Sheriffs' Feasts, and Taunton-dean Ladies. 'This, Madam, is wonderful charming. This, Madam, is so diverting a Silk. This, Madam, – my stars! – how cool it looks! But this, Madam – ye Gods! would I had 10,000 yards of it.' Then gathers up a Sleeve, and places it to our Shoulders. 'It suits your Ladyship's face wonderfully well.' These Fellows are positively the greatest Fops in the Kingdom; they have their Toilets and their fine Night-gowns; their *Chocolate in the Morning*, and their *green Tea two hours after*; Turkey-polts for their Dinner; and their Perfumes, Washes, and clean Linen, equip them for the Parade.

Fanny Burney's *Evelina* describes a shopping expedition with Mrs Mirvan:

The shops are really very entertaining, especially the mercers; there seem to be six or seven men belonging to each shop; and everyone took a care, by bowing and smirking, to be noticed. . . . We were conducted from one to another, and carried from room to room with so much ceremony, that at first I was almost afraid to go on. . . . At the milliners, what most diverted me was, that we were more frequently served by men than by women, and such men! So finical, so affected: they seemed to understand every part of a woman's dress better than

we do ourselves; and they recommended caps and ribbons with an air of so much importance, that I wished to ask them how long they had left off wearing them.

In fact, as distinct from fiction, we have evidence from Robert Owen, early socialist and philanthropist, of shop-assistant dandyism at Flint & Palmer's of London Bridge in the 1780s when, 'boy as I was, I had to wait my turn for the hairdresser to powder and pomatum and curl my hair, for I had two large curls on each side, and a stiff pigtail, and until all this was very nicely and systematically done, no-one could think of appearing before a customer.' Robert Owen had been apprenticed to a draper in Stamford, Lincolnshire, before he came to Flint & Palmer's about 1786 at the age of fifteen.

I was lodged and boarded in the house and had a salary of twenty-five pounds a year, and I thought myself rich and independent. To the assistants in this busy establishment, the duties were very onerous. They were up and had breakfasted and were dressed to receive customers in the shop at 8 o'clock – and dressing then was no slight affair. . . . Between eight and nine the shop began to fill with purchasers, and their number increased until it was crowded to excess, although a large apartment, and this continued until late in the evening; usually until ten, or half-past ten, during all the spring months. Dinner and tea were hastily taken . . . two or three, sometimes only one, escaping at a time to take what he or she could most easily swallow. When the purchasers left at ten or half-past ten, there

43

was work to be performed with closed doors. . . . Frequently at two in the morning, after being actively engaged on foot all day from 8 o'clock in the previous morning, I have scarcely been able with the aid of the banisters to go upstairs to bed. And then I had but five hours sleep. When the spring trade ceased, and the business became less onerous, we could take our meals with some comfort, and retire to rest between eleven and twelve, and by comparison this became an easy life.

The slackening of business when the Season was over was more dramatic in fashionable St James's. Parliament dispersed, the Court moved out to Hampton, the landed aristocrats returned to their country seats, and the people of fascination repaired to their villas at Twickenham, Richmond and other Thames-side paradises. Before they left London, county families did a great deal of shopping for the months to come – stocking up at Fortnum & Mason with tea, coffee and other special groceries, spices and condiments, re-stocking their linen presses and china cupboards, renewing furnishings for their country houses, ordering new riding habits and boots. Often they shopped also for neighbouring families who did not come to town. London was England's great luxury emporium, whose goods carried a cachet no provincial shops could emulate.

In the City, trade was not quite so seasonal, since many of the retail shops, particularly the drapers, acted also as wholesalers. Daniel Defoe again:

As London is the centre of trade, so all the manufactures are brought hither, and from hence circulated again to all the country. Country shopkeepers do not go or send to all the several counties where those goods are made – that is to say, to this part for the cloth, or to that for the lining, to another for buttons, and to another for the thread; but they again correspond with the wholesale dealers in London, where there are particular shops or warehouses for all these; and they not only furnish the country shopkeepers, but give them large credit.

Defoe's book was intended as a retailers' guide, and he emphasized the importance of choosing the right site when setting up shop:

Many trades have their peculiar streets, and proper places for the sale of their goods, where people expect to find such shops, and consequently, when they want such goods, they go thither for them; as the booksellers in St Paul's Churchyard, about the Exchange, Temple, and the Strand etc., the mercers on both sides of Ludgate, in Round Court, and Gracechurch and Lombard Streets; the shoemakers in St Martin's le Grand, and Shoemaker Row; the coachmakers in Long-acre, Queen Street, and Bishopsgate; butchers in Eastcheap; and suchlike. For a tradesman to open his shop in a place unresorted to, or in a place where his trade is not agreeable, and where it is not expected, it is no wonder he has no trade. It is true we have seen a kind of fate attend the very streets and rows where such trades have been gathered together; and a street, famous some years ago, shall, in a few years after, be quite forsaken. Whenever the principal shopkeepers remove, the rest soon follow – knowing, that if the fame of the trade is not there, the customers will not resort thither; and that a tradesman's business is to follow wherever the trade leads.

Many of the names of City streets reflect the one-time congregation of trades in them – Bread Street, Milk Street, Cornhill, Fish Street Hill, the

Poultry, the Vintners, Honey Lane, Hosier Lane, Cordwainer Street, Wood Street. Outside the City, there was one trade which persisted in one particular street, a short distance from Covent Garden, well into the twentieth century. Monmouth Street, running through the notorious Seven Dials, became known as 'Rag Fair' because of the predominance of 'brokers' shops' selling secondhand clothes, boots and shoes. The footwear was usually stocked in cellar shops, reached by a flight of steps from the pavement. Most of the stock in brokers' shops was stolen, received from highwaymen, house-breakers, pilfering servants and workmen, shopworkers and shoplifters. In the seventeenth and eighteenth centuries, when there was great extravagance in dress, men and women of fashion in temporary money difficulties often bought and sold clothes in Monmouth Street. Similarly, young men from good homes in the country, coming to London at the start of their careers, would equip themselves in Monmouth Street with the kind of City clothes deemed necessary. Further down the secondhand scale, a small street near Drury Lane was given over to open shops or stalls belonging to piece-brokers, who bought garments from old clothes men and cut out the soundest pieces of cloth to sell to jobbing tailors for use as patches. The most unsavoury cast-off clothing market was in Whitechapel. Ned Ward wrote that it went by the sweet name of Rosemary Lane because of the 'fragrant fumes that arise from musty rotten rags and burnt old shoes'.

On the corner of Monmouth Street, John West, 'Hat Maker at The Beaver and Star', conducted an enterprising business renting hats by the year, the rental including servicing. His trade-card explained his business as 'Furnishing Gentlemen with the Loan of 3 good new Hats in the Year kept in proper Repair for 15s and upwards to £1.1s, each warranted worth within 3s of the Sum agreed for.' He was, in effect, a forerunner of Moses Moses, who a century later, in 1881, fixed upon a permanent address for his secondhand clothes and hiring business (later Moss Bros.) in King Street, Covent Garden, very near Monmouth Street, the old Rag Fair.

George Cruikshank drew Monmouth Street for Charles Dickens (left). Known as Rag Fair, it was the most profitable beat for the seller of old clothes (right) over a long period.

4 The pattern of eighteenth-century shopping – London town and village

The sign of the Three Pigeons, c. *1750.* Opposite: *Shopping and dalliance, a frequent combination. The date is 1772, the venue almost certainly the New Exchange.*

THE WEALTHY HOUSEHOLDS of eighteenth-century St James's were 'waited upon' by Fortnum & Mason, or by Berry's, for groceries and wine. The daily marketing for meat, fish and vegetables was done by the servants in St James's Market. Gentlemen of fashion and position could order their clothes at London's most exclusive hatters, bootmakers, tailors, hosiers and shirtmakers, all established in this elite male preserve. But there were no fashion shops at all for the wives and daughters of St James's residents. Covent Garden was their nearest shopping venue, with Tavistock Street claiming the most elegant establishments, including Jackson's Habit Warehouse, Paulin's Haberdashery and Pearson the Laceman. Across the Strand, the New Exchange offered all kinds of frivolous falbalas, and in the Strand itself there was a range of fashion shops.

Mrs Hussey, sacque and mantua-maker, was the formidable aunt of J. T. Smith, who describes her in his biography of the sculptor Joseph Nollekens, 1737–1823. Mrs Hussey lived to be 105 and had four husbands. On the death of Mr Hussey, her second husband, she set up shop in the Strand 'a few doors west of the celebrated Le Beck, a famous cook who had a large portrait of himself for the sign of his house'. Henry Fielding immortalized Mrs Hussey when describing Sophia Western: 'Such charms are there in affability, and so sure is it to attract the praises of all kinds of people. It may, indeed, be compared to the celebrated Mrs Hussey.' J. T. Smith has it that Fielding had promised to introduce Mrs Hussey into his novel, but forgot his promise until after the manuscript had gone to the printers. There was just time to rush along and insert the reference in Volume II, with the note: 'A celebrated mantua-maker in the Strand, famous for setting off the shapes of women'.

Nollekens' mother used to take her children for haircuts during the 1740s to a barber in the Strand known as Bat Pidgeon, whose house bore the sign of Three Pigeons. And she may well have taken them sometimes to Exeter Change, famous for its toys. It was built in 1676 on the site of Lord Burleigh's mansion, Exeter House, on the north side of the Strand about where the Strand Palace Hotel is now. Robert Southey described it in his *Letters from England* as 'precisely a Bazaar, a sort of street under cover, or large long room, with a row of shops on either hand, and a

thoroughfare between them; the shops being furnished with such articles as might tempt an idler, or remind a passenger of his wants – walking-sticks, implements for shaving, knives, scissors, watch-chains, purses, etc.' It seems a bizarre background for the lying-in-state of the much-beloved poet John Gay before his burial in Westminster Abbey in 1732, even though Gay had begun life as a silk mercer's apprentice in the Strand. But at least there was no menagerie in Exeter Change then, for this was not to be inaugurated until the 1770s. Lord William Pitt Lennox recalled visiting it as a child in the early nineteenth century:

Often have I gazed on the gaudy appearance of the beefeaters, in their gorgeous red and gold liveries, listened to the roars, cries, groans, screeches, yells, and screams of the lions, tigers, panthers, monkeys and birds: cast wistful eye over the well-stocked counters, the bats, balls, kites, hoops of the toyshop, and revelled in the Bath buns, blanc-manges, jellies, tartlets, sponge-cakes, of the pastry cooks.

For household provisions, the Strand had Hungerford Market. The spendthrift Sir Edward Hungerford thought to recoup his fortune by pulling down his riverside mansion and building a market on the site – a successful speculation, as it turned out. When Dr Johnson said, 'Fleet Street has a very animated appearance, but I think that the full tide of human existence is at Charing Cross', he was referring to the busy, popular Hungerford market and its environs. The market was rebuilt by a private company in 1833, with splendid new facilities which included a footbridge over the Thames: but soon it had to be demolished to make way for Charing Cross Station. The Hungerford footbridge remains.

James Lackington's shop in Finsbury Square: a reflection of the growth in book sales at the end of the eighteenth century.

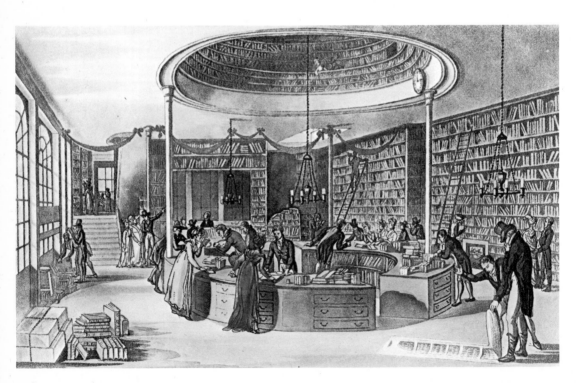

It was in a Covent Garden bookshop that Boswell's momentous first meeting with Dr Johnson took place: to be precise, in the back parlour of Thomas Davies's shop in Russell Street. In King Street, nearby, was Francis Noble's Circulating Library at the sign of Otway's Head. Boswell referred to an occasion when he had left a guinea security at Noble's; and when he was confined to his lodgings with 'the pox', he wrote: 'Noble also sends me from time to time a fresh supply of novels from his circulating library, so that I am very well provided with entertainment.' One wonders whether Noble included amongst them John Cleland's notorious *Memoirs of a Woman of Pleasure,* generally known as *Fanny Hill.* Boswell wrote on 31 March 1772 that he had met at Garrick's house 'old Cleland, in his youth the author of *The Woman of Pleasure*, that most licentious and inflaming book' – a description that implies he had himself read it. Another of Boswell's booksellers was Alexander Donaldson, whose shop was on the corner of Arundel Street, Strand. Boswell called him 'the Great', 'the Immense', and 'the Illustrious', because of his ambitious publishing schemes and his lordly manner.

When Boswell and his friend Erskine were having a volume of their letters to each other published, Boswell went with Alexander Donaldson 'to the booksellers in Paternoster Row, whom he engaged to befriend us. In these matters the favour of *the trade* (as the booksellers call themselves) is a prodigious point.' Boswell, while feeling himself socially superior to 'the trade' (was he not the son of a Scottish earl?) condescended to have a merry evening at the Queen's head in Holborn

with Chandler my printer and Flexney my bookseller. We had a bit of supper, and every man drank his bottle of Rhenish with sugar. Flexney is a fine, smart, obliging, merry little man, and Chandler an honest, well-behaved, good-humoured, laughing fellow. I thought an evening of this kind very proper after our *Letters* were fairly published. They admired me much and I gave them all encouragement. We were very good friends and very lively and chatty. . . . The connection between authors, printers, and booksellers must be kept up.

Francis Noble's Circulating Library in Covent Garden lent books in English and French 'At Half a Guinea a Year' or 'Three Shillings a Quarter' (left). Hatchard's, established at No. 187 Piccadilly in 1797, is still there. This Edwardian photograph shows books opened for window display – in those days there were no colourful book jackets.

49

Shopping in the Strand. A money-lender was to be found close to St Mary's Church in 1796 (above). More cultural was Ackermann's Repository of Arts at No. 96 (above right). Hungerford Market provided household provisions (right); and after its rebuilding in 1833, the opening ceremony (far right) proved to be a gala occasion.

James Lackington, a bookseller at The Temple of the Muses, Chiswell Street, Finsbury Square, wrote in his *Memoirs*, published in 1792:

I suppose that more than four times the number of books are sold now than were sold twenty years since. The poorer sort of farmers, and even the poor country people in general, who before that period spent their winter evenings in relating stories of hob-goblins etc. now shorten their winter nights by hearing their sons and daughters read tales, romances, etc; and on entering their houses, you may see *Tom Jones*, *Roderick Random*, and other entertaining books stuck up on the bacon racks, etc. If John goes to town with a load of hay, he is charged to be sure not to forget to bring home *Peregrine Pickle's* adventures; and when Dolly is sent to market to sell her eggs, she is commissioned to purchase *The History of Pamela Andrews*. In short, all ranks and degrees now READ.

James Lackington had started his bookshop without capital, buying secondhand books a few at a time. Later he travelled as far as the West Country to buy private libraries, sending back waggon loads of books to his partner. He averred his plan had always been to 'give as much for libraries as it is possible for a tradesman to give, and sell them and *new* publications also, for the same *small profits* that have been attended with such astonishing success for some years past'. He saw his shop as a place for the diffusion of knowledge: 'Among all the schools where the knowledge of mankind is to be acquired, I know of none equal to that of a bookseller's shop, especially if the master is of an inquisitive and communicative turn and is in a considerable line of business. His shop will then be a place of resort for men, women and children, of various nations, and more of various capacities, dispositions, etc.'

When on 30 June 1797, John Hatchard opened the bookshop which still trades under his name in the same premises, he wrote in his diary: 'This day, by the grace of God, the goodwill of my friends, and £5 in my pocket, I have opened my bookshop in Piccadilly.' Discriminating bibliophiles and wealthy residents of what he called 'this small London suburb' soon made a habit of dropping in to look at the latest publications, enjoy a cup of coffee and a chat in what Hatchard spoke of as his 'literary coffee shop'.

The originator of circulating libraries is said by Henry Curwen in his *History of Booksellers* to have been a bookseller named Wright, who established his library at 132 Strand 'about 1730'. Other authorities have credited William Bathoe 'At the Bible near Exeter 'Change in the Strand' with being the first, as late as 1743. A place in the first three must surely be given to the Rev. Samuel Fancourt, a dissenting minister, who set up, about 1740, the Universal Library in Crane Court, Fleet Street, announcing: 'The Gentlemen and Ladies' Growing and Circulating Library. Membership one guinea a year.' From 1765, John Newbery's Juvenile Library in St Paul's Churchyard was a great place for children to be taken to visit 'their old friend' Mr Newbery. His sixpenny publications, gaily bound in flowered and gilt paper, were more durable than the crude chapbooks (just folded, not stitched), which had previously been the only children's books. Later there was Godwin's Juvenile Library, conceived by Mrs Godwin (Mary Wollstonecraft) and

first established in Hanway Street, moving two years later to 41 Skinner Street. From there, under the imprint M. J. Godwin, were published most of Mary and Charles Lamb's books for children.

Ackermann's Repository of Arts in 1809, extended from No. 96 Strand to No. 101.

In 1771, Rudolf Ackermann from Germany opened a print shop in the Strand, opposite Exeter Change. He called it Ackermann's Repository of Arts, and held evening receptions once a week when fashionable people gathered to view his prints and converse with others of the *ton*. From 1809 to 1829 he published a monthly periodical given the same name as the shop, a faultless production containing exquisite colour prints dealing with the decorative arts: furnishings and furniture, dress, carriages, all the appurtenances of elegant living. His son, also Rudolf, was one of the first lessees in Regent Street, opening in 1826 a print shop at No. 191 independently of his father.

John Bell began his business in the Strand about 1780 as a distributor of French books, calling it the British Library. By January 1787 he was advertising his Subscription Library as including 'English Publications, and every sort of publication which shall appear in Paris from this day'. Dr Burney, historian of music and father of Fanny Burney, was a subscriber to Bell's Library. In emulation of Ackermann, John Bell in 1805 opened a 'Gallery of Arts' in Southampton Street, where he held exhibitions and sold books and prints. The following year he began a monthly magazine almost as beautifully produced and illustrated as

53

Ackermann's *Repository of the Arts*, although the text dealt chiefly with dress fashions and Society tittle-tattle. He called it *La Belle Assemblée* and it continued until 1837, edited from 1832 by the beautiful and witty Caroline Norton.

Other print shops opened in different parts of London in response to the interest a wider public was showing in politics and foreign affairs. National events provided occasions for commemorative work, and exhibitions of prints became social occasions almost as fashionable as exhibitions of paintings in the later eighteenth century; and for the man and woman on the pavements, print-shop windows provided free picture galleries. At 148 Strand, Messrs. Leigh and Sotheby ran a book and print shop as well as operating their auction rooms. In 1786, Sophie von la Roche noted in her London diary: 'I saw a number of people standing near an engraver's, in front of some caricatures, the subject of which was the life and marriage of the Prince of Wales; they are sold to the public. We also saw some portraits of Count Cagliostro and his wife and numerous reproductions of the royal family.'

Count Cagliostro was a very fashionable quack doctor. Frau von la Roche went to visit him 'in Knightsbridge, one of London's outermost suburbs, in a new well-equipped house, with large tracts of meadow-land and low, lopped trees beside a winding stream in front of it.' This stream was the Tyburn, flowing down to the Thames. Tyburn Lane, later named Park Lane, was the western boundary of the metropolis. Kensington, two miles further along the highroad to the west than the hamlet of Knightsbridge, was of course totally detached from London. Frau von la Roche described it as 'a lovely village full of wealthy people . . . many inhabitants of London who have no country seats of their own, in summer move into Kensington houses for the sake of the good air, the gardens and the fine prospect'. Boswell's friend Dempster took country lodgings there for himself and his sister, and Boswell enjoyed walking out to dine with them – 'He is charmingly lodged here, and the fellow enjoys it much.'

The village had experienced its period of importance when King William III bought the Earl of Nottingham's house in 1691 and Wren transformed it into Kensington Palace. There was great need of houses for people of various positions attached to the Court, and a builder named Thomas Young, who had already begun to lay out a small residential square on land he had bought just south of the Great Western Road, hastened to complete it. To reverse a phrase, this Kensington Square might be called *Urbs in Rure*. Faulkner, in his *History and Antiquities of Kensington*, wrote: 'While the Court was held at Kensington, most of the houses were inhabited by persons of quality. Ambassadors, Gentry, and Clergy, and at one time upwards of forty carriages were kept in and about the neighbourhood. In the time of George II, the demand for lodgings was so great that an Ambassador, a Bishop, and a Physician have been known to occupy apartments in the same house.'

Naturally, with all this 'quality' to bestow their custom, there was what Bowack described in his *Antiquities of Middlesex* as 'an abundance of shop-keepers and all sorts of artificers in it, which makes it appear rather like part of London, than a country village'. But when George III, on his accession in 1760, moved the Court to Buckingham House, the shopkeepers dealing in luxury goods soon disappeared, leaving just the little shops that supplied daily necessities for the permanent residents. Kensington became a village once more. It was not only distance that divided it from London, but danger. The stretch of the Great Western Road between Kensington and Hyde Park Corner toll-gate was a haunt of highwaymen and footpads. When the Court was at Kensington, carriages were advised to go through Hyde Park in armed convoy, and a patrol of Guards was set up for the safe passage of those leaving the Palace gaming tables at night. Later, 300 lamps were set along the way through the parks from Kensington Palace to St James's; but the cost of the oil was so great that they were only lit in winter. In 1740 the *Gentleman's Magazine* contained an item: 'The Bristol Mail from London was robbed a little beyond Knightsbridge by a man on foot, who took the Bath and Bristol bags, and mounting the Post-boy's horse, rode off towards London.' The mail coach team seems to have put up a poor resistance, if any, to the one man on foot. Horace Walpole, who was robbed in full daylight in Hyde Park by the 'Gentleman Highwayman' (a Presbyterian Minister's son named James McLean), expostulated that one 'was forced to travel even at noon as if one was going into battle . . . what a shambles this country is grown!' As late as 1821, Lady Holland in a letter to her son when she was expecting Lord Holland back from Ampthill wrote: 'Dear Papa will return, I trust, before footpad hour.'

Hyde Park Corner toll-gate was removed in 1825, the year short-stage coaches started. About 600 of these coaches made some 1,800 journeys daily between the City and Westminster and outlying villages such as

Kensington Church Street and St Mary Abbott's, with the village stocks, c. 1750.

Kensington, Hampstead, Highgate, Hammersmith and Chiswick. They supplied a convenient form of public transport which made it possible for gentlemen who did not own their own carriages to travel to their place of business each day from a house in pleasant rural surroundings, and for their womenfolk to make frequent forays to the West End shopping streets.

The most favoured village to the north of London was Islington, to which many City men from the mid-seventeenth century onwards removed their families to benefit by the clean air high above the City smoke. Surrounded by pastures on which cattle supplying milk to the metropolis grazed, Islington was famous for its cream and cakes. London citizens loved to walk out to its tea-gardens with their wives or sweethearts on a summer Sunday. In the last decade of the century there was considerable building of pleasant middle-class property, and Islington was becoming what in later times became known as a 'dormitory suburb'. As early as 1665 John Playford was a commuter. He had his shop and press for music publishing in the Inner Temple, and rented a large house in Upper Street, Islington. There his wife conducted a boarding school, while he travelled daily to the Temple. Canonbury House, originally belonging to the priors of St Bartholomew's, was rebuilt later as the country mansion of the Duke of Northumberland, but after the Civil War the house and its separate tower were rented in apartments. In the eighteenth century, most of the tenants were connected with politics and literature. John Newbery, the publisher, lived there with his family, and installed Oliver Goldsmith in a separate apartment. There he was visited by Boswell on 27 June 1763 –

Hyde Park Corner, c. 1750. The apple stall by the Park gate was kept by an old woman who claimed squatting rights when Lord Apsley wanted to build his house (later the residence of the Duke of Wellington). She sat tight until bought out at what was rumoured to be a vast sum.

'I then walked out to Islington and went to Canonbury House, a curious old monastic building, now let out in lodgings, where Dr Goldsmith stays.'

More traffic came to the village when London's first by-pass, the New Road from Paddington to Islington, was constructed in 1755–6. And later an aura of romance arrived with the stage coaches. The Peacock Inn at Islington was the first stop out of London for the northern coaches which started from The Bull and Mouth at St Martin's-le-Grand. New shops opened near the Peacock to serve travellers, and more middle-class streets and squares were developed. But the highways leading to the City were still dangerous to people travelling in their own carriages and to lone horse riders. Charles Lamb, whose mother was an Islington butcher's daughter, lived twice during his adult life at different Islington addresses with his sister Mary. In a letter of 1798 he related how his tailor was driving from Hampstead with his wife and family in a one-horse shay when they were robbed 'of four guineas, some shillings and halfpence, and a bundle of customers' measures, which they swore were banknotes. They did not shoot him, and when they rode off he addrest them with profound gratitude, making a congee: "Gentlemen, I wish you good night, and we are very much obliged to you that you have not used us ill!"'

North Country mails at the Peacock Inn, Islington; Chapman's apothecary shop and a sweet shop alongside.

5 Residential Soho and its specialist shops

SOHO HAD ARRIVED on the fashionable map by the end of the seventeenth century. The westward thrust of society had crossed St Martin's Lane, the boundary of the Covent Garden area, and transformed Leicester Fields into a residential square. Between Leicester Square in the south and the Oxford Road in the north lay Soho Fields. It was an area that had gradually been built over despite a proclamation of 1671 prohibiting 'the erecting of small habitations and cottages in the fields called the Windmill Fields, Dog's Fields, and the fields adjoining to So-Hoe' which, it declared, 'choak up the air of His Majesty's palaces and parks'.

The development which transformed this squalid area into a fashionable quarter began in 1681 when a handsome mansion was built to Wren's design for the Duke of Monmouth, putative son of Charles II. An elegant roué, romantic adventurer and pretender to the throne, he bestowed glamour upon the new square of fine houses laid out in front of his own mansion and named King's Square. Only four years after the mansion's completion came the Battle of Sedgemoor and Monmouth's execution; but Soho Square, as King's Square was subsequently named, was well established as an elegant address, and tenants of Monmouth House included several French Ambassadors before it was demolished in 1773. As a quarter, Soho attracted London's foreign communities, and at one time Poland Street had three foreign legations. There were also literary connections. The Turk's Head at No. 9 Gerrard Street was the venue for Dr Johnson's Literary Club, whose members included Joshua Reynolds, Goldsmith, Garrick, Burke and Boswell. Hazlitt lived in Frith Street, and Addison sited Sir Roger de Coverley's lodgings in Soho. Both Mrs Thrale (before her marriage) and Mrs Chapone lived in Dean Street, and Elizabeth Inchbald, celebrated actress and dramatist, was living in a single room in Frith Street when writing her first novel *A Simple Story* during 1791.

The most notorious resident was Mrs Cornelys, sometimes called the Sultana of Soho. Born in Venice the daughter of an actor, she had a chequered career before enshrining herself in Carlisle House, Soho Square, in 1760. She had it magnificently decorated and held subscription balls, concerts, 'Society Nights' and masquerades which

A Design for a State Bed.

T. Chippendale invt et delin.   Published according to Act of Parliament. 1761.

were a sensational success with the *haut ton*. At one masquerade the Duchess of Kingston appeared as Phigenia in what Horace Walpole described as 'a state almost ready for the sacrifice'. On another evening, a reveller was reported to have appeared as 'Adam in flesh-coloured silk with an apron of fig-leaves'. Carlisle House was grist to the gossip-writers' mills for many years. But, like all fashions, it went out of fashion. The entertainments came to an end by the early 1780s. Mrs Cornelys made one subsequent effort to attract attention by setting herself up as a vendor of asses' milk in a suite of frivolously embellished rooms in Knightsbridge, inviting the beau monde to breakfast. She died a debtor in the Fleet Prison.

In 1816 a shopping bazaar was opened in Soho Square. It was planned and financed by a benevolent Mr John Trotter with the motive of helping widows and daughters of men lost in the Napoleonic Wars. Stalls were let at a rental of $1\frac{1}{4}$d per square foot per day to applicants who could supply references of good moral character. There was a large kitchen and dining-room at the back of the building where stallholders were served with inexpensive refreshments. The motive behind the enterprise encouraged the good-will of Society, and long after its charitable beginnings were forgotten the Soho Bazaar continued to attract upper-class customers. Charles Knight wrote of it in 1851:

Stalls or open counters range on both sides of aisles or passages, on two separate floors of the building. The articles sold are almost exclusively pertaining to the dress and personal decoration of ladies and children; such as millinery, lace, gloves, jewellery, etc; and, in the height of 'the season', the long array of carriages drawn up near the building testifies to the extent of the visits paid by the high-born and wealthy to this place. Some of the rules of the establishment are very stringent. A plain and modest style of dress on the part of the young females who serve at the stalls is invariably insisted on, a matron being at hand to superintend the whole.

The individual shops in Soho were mainly those of craftsmen making and selling their own wares, wholesale as well as retail. The Brontës' piano in the parsonage at Haworth was made by John Green of Soho Square. Chippendale's first workshop was at No. 60 St Martin's Lane, the eastern boundary of Soho. French and Swiss watchmakers and jewellers occupied most of Church Street; and in Gerrard Street there was 'Le Grand, Pastry-cook and Cook' – most pastry cooks and confectioners in London at this time were French or Swiss. Also in Gerrard Street, Dryden's old house was taken in 1790 by Atkinson the perfumer. He placed a life-size stuffed bear in the doorway to advertise the firm's principal product, bear's grease for gentlemen's luxuriant hair. This was distilled, if that is the word, in the cellar below the shop. When Atkinson's moved to Old Bond Street in 1832, the stuffed bear was not welcomed by the fastidious Bond Street shopkeepers. So he had to be retired. As a shop-sign, he had been akin to the life-size wooden Highlanders who frequently stood in the doorways of tobacconists' shops. It is thought that this custom was begun by David Wishart of Coventry Street in the early eighteenth century, to indicate that he sold

Scots snuff as distinct from Bristol snuff; but life-size Highlanders, their dress painted in the colours of famous Highland regiments, became one of the most usual tobacconists' signs. In *Little Dorrit*, Dickens wrote: 'The tobacco business round the corner of Horsemonger Lane was of too modest a character to support a life-size Highlander, but it maintained a little one on a bracket on the door post, who looked like a fallen cherub that had found it necessary to take to a kilt.' When Highland dress was made illegal after the rebellion of 1745, there were jokes about the 'illegally dressed' figures at tobacconists' shops – but there were no prosecutions.

Two shop-signs that have survived into modern times are those of the pawnbroker's three balls, and the barber's pole. The original barbers' poles were painted red, because barbers were often surgeons as well; and from the pole hung a gallipot, or bleeding dish, to indicate that 'cupping' was undertaken. When white stripes were added to the red poles, they were said to represent linen bandages. R. Campbell wrote in his *The London Tradesman*:

The Barber's trade was formerly connected with that of a Surgeon, and Numbers of them in London and Westminster let Blood and draw Teeth. I cannot too much condemn the Folly of trusting these Bunglers to perform one of the nicest, tho' common Operations in Surgery. . . . I never saw a good Surgeon, but was under some Apprehension when he was about to let Blood; yet these Fellows for Threepence, break a Vein at random, without the least Hesitation.

Sir Ambrose Heal's collection of eighteenth-century trade-cards includes that of 'Samuel Darkin ye elder, Operator of Teeth and Samuel Darkin the younger, Bleeder and Operator of Teeth; also cups at the Sign of the Bleeder and Star'. Mr Darkin was Surgeon Dentist to His Majesty, but any citizen could call at the Sign of the Bleeder and Star and pay to have a tooth drawn or to be bled – a sanguinary process thought necessary for countless conditions, from apoplexy to gout or a headache. During the 1770s a lady dentist named Mrs de St Raymond advertised in

William Conaway of Soho who 'furnished Persons of Quality with Lamps, Lanthorns & Irons' emphasised the cachet of his clients on his trade card (left). It depicts the Duke of Monmouth's mansion, designed by Sir Christopher Wren, having its lamps serviced by Conaway's employees; while (right) the trade card of Samuel Darkin, Surgeon Dentist to His Majesty, makes it clear by the fair client depicted that he 'also cups at the Sign of the Bleeder & Star'.

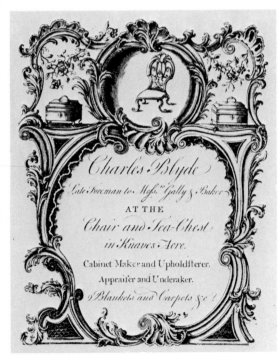

Sir William Hamilton (top), husband of Nelson's Lady Hamilton, George III (above left) and Admiral Keppel (above right) were included in Wedgwood's Famous Heads series. His showrooms were moved from Soho to York Street, St James's Square, when Ackermann's Repository of Arts *featured them in 1809 (above, far right). Charles Blyde (left) was another craftsman/tradesman of Soho. His premises were in Knave's Acre, Golden Square, described by Strype as 'chiefly inhabited by those that deal in old goods and glass bottles'.*

the *Morning Post*. The public was informed of 'the lightness of her hand in removing all tartarous concretions, so destructive to the teeth, and her dexterity in extracting stumps, splits, and fangs of teeth. . . . She makes and fixes in artificial teeth . . . and transplants teeth from the jaws of poor lads into the heads of any lady or gentleman.' Dentistry skills, or bunglings, were sometimes exercised by barbers; and when Nollekens lived in Soho as a boy, a near neighbour was D. R. Ritchie, hairdresser and dentist of Rupert Street.

One very grand establishment in Soho was the retail showroom of Josiah Wedgwood of Staffordshire. He had first opened London showrooms in 1765, rather surprisingly in Grosvenor Square – surprisingly because one would not expect retail premises to have been permitted in that aristocratic residential square, described by its historian Arthur Dasent as 'strewn with the strawberry leaves and blue ribbons of the Garter'. The showrooms were so successful that after only two years Wedgwood was looking for larger premises. Pall Mall was suggested to him, but he considered it to be 'too accessible to the common Folk . . . for you know that my present Sett of Customers will not mix with the Rest of the World'. It is perplexing that he should have turned down Pall Mall, of all streets, as insufficiently exclusive; but he could have been influenced by the fact that the proprietor of Chelsea Porcelain, Nicholas Sprimont, had opened a retail shop in Pall Mall in 1752 and then moved to Piccadilly only five years later. At any rate, it was on the corner of Newport Street and St Martin's Lane that Wedgwood established his London warehouse in 1767.

Wedgwood was a great salesman and showman as well as a great potter. By means of well-advertised exhibitions, with personal invitation cards for the private-views, he drew in fashionable and artistic coteries. The most publicized exhibition was that of the dinner service for Catherine the Great of Russia in 1774. New rooms were taken at Portland House, 13 Greek Street, and admittance to the opening was by invitation only. Thereafter, day after day for over a month, or so it was reported, the carriages of the nobility and gentry, even of royalty, blocked the narrow streets of Soho. Commemorative pieces were another great draw: the rise of Methodism, the Slave Trade controversy, the Peace with France, were all given ceramic expression; while Wedgwood's 'Famous Heads' series of Greeks and Romans was given topical interest by the addition of heads of contemporary celebrities: Dr Johnson, David Garrick, Mrs Siddons, Captain Cook. The 'Famous Country Seats' service naturally attracted the owners of the country houses depicted to see it, however distant they were from London. This service was evidently being exhibited when Frau von la Roche visited the Wedgwood showrooms in 1786: 'At Wedgwood's to-day I saw a thousand lovely forms and images; vases, tea-things, statuettes, medallions, seals, tableware and a service on which pictures of the finest villas and gardens of the last three reigns were painted.' Below stairs, in the lower shop, were the less expensive pieces. For these Wedgwood planned something akin to modern self-service in that he ordered the pieces be displayed 'where people can come at them and serve themselves'.

The new fashion for tea-drinking was a factor in the swelling sales of all potteries at this time. Everybody now needed a tea set for polite entertaining. Wedgwood extended his market to include 'the common folk' by offering tea things in a range of prices from fine china for the aristocracy down to inexpensive ware for the lower middle class. Tea-drinking was a fashion that spread down the social scale with amazing rapidity considering the astronomical cost of tea; and unlike most fashionable crazes it was not abandoned by the upper classes when the lower orders had taken it up. China shops opened all over London selling tea sets, and until the end of the century it was usual for these shops to sell tea and coffee as well. R. Campbell, in his *The London*

Tradesman, called china shops Earthenware Shops, and wrote:

They generally deal in Tea, Coffee, and Chocolate. They buy the Goods from several Houses in England, from Holland, and at the Sales of the East-India Company. It they trade in Tea, it requires a large Stock to set up with; because at the East-India Sales they can buy nothing less than a Lot, which generally amounts to about three or four Hundred Pounds; the smaller Traders in this Way are obliged to join two or three together to buy a Lot.

Tea, coffee and chocolate were also included in the stock of high-class grocers, and other trades turned the new fashion to their advantage. The *Post Man* of 10 March 1711 announced 'Isaac Van den Helm, a Dutch Tablemaker over against Compton Street by Ann's Wall, next to the Golden Key, Soho, makes and sells all sorts of fine painted Tea Tables, with new fancies, and that endure boiling hot water.'

All through the eighteenth century the consumption of tea increased, and there were kill-joys who complained that the habit of tea-drinking was as demoralizing to the working classes as gin-drinking had been earlier. At the beginning of the nineteenth century the magnitude of the tea trade was wondered at by Miss Weeton, the lonely schoolteacher from Lancashire, when she was staying at Mrs Benson's in George Terrace, Commercial Road: 'From seventy to eighty caravans, each as large as those which usually convey wild beasts, are passing daily to the East India Docks, and return filled with tea to the India House.' Miss Weeton was shocked by finding shops open on Sundays: 'All the way as I go to any place of Worship, fruit stalls are in the road, and confectioners' shops open, as on any other day. I wonder much at it; I never saw it so glaringly elsewhere.' The only things that could *legally* be sold on Sundays were milk and mackerel – 'E'en Sundays are prophan'd by Mackrell Cries', wrote John Gay. Not, in very truth, that he was one to be shocked.

A lively tea-garden at the height of the tea-drinking fashion.

Oxford Street: a map of its surroundings in 1801;
towards the east end of the street the Pantheon (left)
designed by James Wyatt for balls and masquerades, but by
the time of this engraving about to become, in 1834, a
shopping bazaar conducted on the lines of the Soho Bazaar;
a view in the 1790s of the countrified Marylebone Road,
then known as the New Road, London's first by-pass
(above right); and Tyburn turnpike at the western
entrance to Oxford Street (above left).

Cavendish House

CLARK & DEBENHAM

Every Article on the same
of the best Quality, Terms as FLINT's.

FOR READY MONEY ONLY

Silk Mercers, Haberdashers,
Hosiers, Milliners, & Lacemen
(Nº 44)
Wigmore St. Cavendish Square.
FAMILY MOURNING.
&c.
A Large & elegant Assortment
of Cotton Twills, Stuffs, Bombazines,
Sarsnets, Satins, Millinery,
Pelisses, & Dresses.

Clark & Debenham, Wigmore Street forerunners of Debenham & Freebody. Opposite: From the stock-in-trade of the eighteenth-century milkman, asses' milk was especially expensive.

6 Oxford Street, and the bright lights of visitors' London

THE NORTHERN boundary of Soho was the King's highway to Oxford. It ran into open country after Tyburn toll-gate, which was approximately where the Marble Arch is now. The stretch of the highway from the toll-gate to Mary-le-bone Lane was called Tyburn Road; from there to Holborn it was called the Oxford Road. Waggons, carts and commercial vehicles rumbled along it ceaselessly and there were said to be more taverns on the mile between Tyburn and Holborn than on any other road in the metropolis. There were also eating houses, or 'ordinaries'. On a spring Sunday in 1763, James Boswell, having been at St Clement's Church, 'which gave me very devout ideas', dined with some misgivings at Chapman's Eating-house in Oxford Road. He needed to assure himself that his choice of street was nothing to do with his perverse attraction to Tyburn Gallows. At another time he confessed to 'a sort of horrid eagerness' to see an execution. This, of course, he succumbed to in the end – climbing up on to some scaffold to get a good view of 'all the dismal scene'.

There were eight hanging days a year, on which workers in most trades were granted a holiday. 'It was common through the whole metropolis', Harry Angelo wrote in his *Reminiscences* in 1828, 'for master coach-makers, frame-makers, tailors, shoe-makers, and others who had engaged to complete orders within a given time, to bear in mind to observe to their customers, "that will be a hanging-day and my men will not be at work".' Citizens lined the route from the Tower or Newgate to Tyburn, jeering and throwing rotten vegetables at the victims, who were drawn in carts. Less humble victims rode in coaches. Highwaymen, the romantic aristocrats of crime, went in gala state, in their finest clothes, accepting bouquets from 'light ladies' and posturing as heroes to the end. There was a permanent wooden grandstand near the gallows, known as Mother Proctor's Pews. Here the 'quality' could, at a price, sit as at a bullfight or the Wimbledon tennis championships. They got a good show for their money, for there could be as many as twenty executions. Street sellers were out in force, hot-potato and chestnut merchants, all the traditional accompaniments of a citizens' day out. And pickpockets, of course: J. T. Smith recorded that Nollekens' father-in-law, a magistrate, had his office thronged the morning after hanging

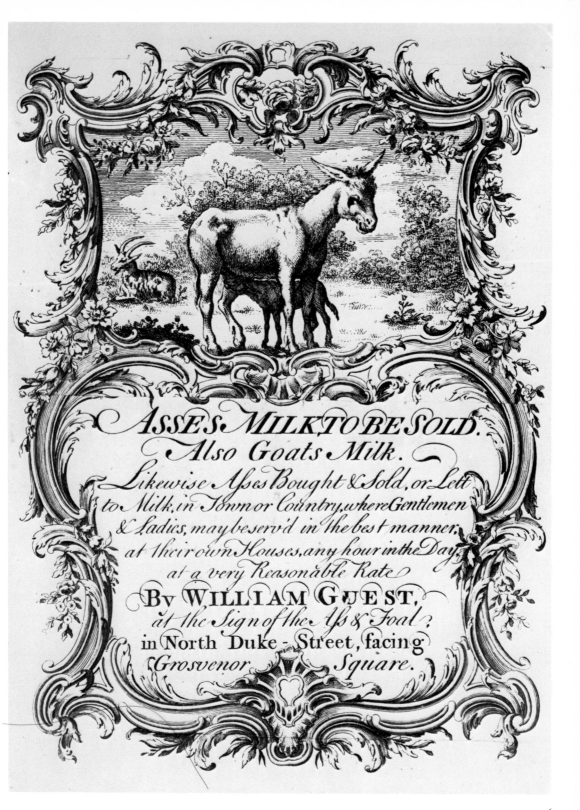

ASSES MILK, TO BE SOLD.
Also Goats Milk.
Likewise Asses Bought & Sold, or Lett
to Milk, in Town or Country, where Gentlemen
& Ladies, may be serv'd in the best manner,
at their own Houses, any hour in the Day,
at a very Reasonable Rate
By WILLIAM GUEST,
at the Sign of the Ass & Foal,
in North Duke - Street, facing
Grosvenor Square.

A City dairy in Golden Lane, 1835.

days 'by gentlemen who had lost their watches and pocket-books, and ladies who had been robbed of their velvet cardinals and purses'.

The Tyburn entertainment ended in 1783, although for some time the gallows were left standing, to be gazed at with pleasurable *frissons*. The number of taverns along the highroad fell, and respectable shops took the place of tawdry booths. There was as yet no depth of building to the north of the road. Mary-le-bone was a separate village, a pleasant place for a Sunday walk. Mr and Mrs Nollekens would sometimes go for an evening stroll to Madame Caria's 'French Gardens', near the end of Mary-le-bone Lane. Here one could, for one penny a head, be accommodated with 'tea equipage and hot-water'. Frugal Mr and Mrs Nollekens would set out with a little tea and sugar, a French roll or a couple of rusks in their pockets.

The marshy pasturage to the east of Mary-le-bone Lane belonged to Robert Harley of Wigmore Castle, Earl of Oxford and Mortimer; and on part of it he had Cavendish Square laid out between 1717 and 1719. But the north side of the square was unfinished when in 1720 the South Sea Bubble halted building; and Harley Street was left to peter out into dank pasturage where wild duck were shot. But the Oxford Market, which was to serve the new residential district, was completed. It was sited on a piece of waste land just north-east of where Oxford Circus came later, behind where Peter Robinson's shop has been since 1833. Designed by James Gibbs, the architect of the estate, the market was a square arcaded building, with a steep roof finished with a weather vane, similar to markets still existing in many country towns. It was demolished in 1880. Today, Market Court and Market Place are reminders of the site.

When the building of the Cavendish-Harley estate was resumed about 1770, alert shopkeepers saw that it would be a good neighbourhood for high-class trading. In Wigmore Street, leading off Cavendish Square, Flint & Clark opened their drapery shop in 1778 – the shop that later became Clark & Debenham, and still later Debenham & Freebody.

Nearly opposite them in Wigmore Street, Thomas Edwards at the Ass & Foal sold milk straight from the ass, as his grandfather had done before him. Asses' milk was almost twice the price of cows' milk, and during the eighteenth century asses were taken round to some big houses to be milked on the doorstep, as John Gay described:

The Oxford Market, designed for local domestic needs, survived until the late nineteenth century.

> *Before proud Gates attending Asses bray,*
> *Or arrogate with solemn Pace the Way;*
> *These grave Physicians with their milky Chear,*
> *The love-sick Maid, and dwindling Beau repair.*

The Donkeys' Dairy at the Tyburn corner of Hyde Park kept some dozen mother asses, bottling their milk for delivery to regular customers, as well as serving it on the premises. Cows' milk, straight from the grazing cow, could also be bought in Hyde Park and the Green Park.

The Oxford Road, decontaminated from the Tyburn connection, fast became a shopping street. Sophie von la Roche, on her London visit in 1786, took an evening walk along it and wrote to her family:

Just imagine, dear children, a street taking half an hour to cover from end to end, with double rows of brightly shining lamps, in the middle of which stands an equally long row of beautifully lacquered coaches and on either side of these there is room for two coaches to pass one another; and the pavement, inlaid with flag-stones, can stand six people deep and allows one to gaze at the splendidly lit shop fronts in comfort. First one passes a watchmaker's, then a silk or fan store, now a silversmith's, a china or glass shop. The spirit booths are particularly tempting, for the English are in any case fond of strong drink. Here crystal flasks of every shape and form are exhibited: each one has a light behind it which makes all the different coloured spirits sparkle. Just as alluring are the confectioners and fruiterers, where, behind the handsome glass windows, pyramids of pineapples, figs, grapes, oranges and all manner of fruits are on show. . . Most of all we admired a stall with Argand and other lamps, situated in a corner-house, and forming a really dazzling spectacle.

These are not the naïve raptures of a wide-eyed girl making her first visit to the largest city in the world. Sophie was then a lady of fifty, wife of the Councillor to the Elector of Mainz. She was a well-known journalist, the first woman to write a novel in Germany, and her friends in literary and artistic circles included Goethe. She came with introductions to many distinguished English people, and was even received at Windsor Castle. She was also what we would call a culture-vulture, eager to learn about, and record, everything she saw. Certainly she was bitten by the Anglomania indulged in by many Germans in the last quarter of the eighteenth century, and was doubtless ready to admire all things English before she ever set foot in England. But she had previously travelled in Europe, and her journal frequently compared London streets and shops favourably with those of Paris and other capital cities.

Sophie even commended London butchers, although at this time, and for half a century after, they were open-fronted to the street, with no protection from flies and the dust created by passing traffic! 'I was glad to strike some of the streets in which the butchers are housed, and interested to find the meat so fine and shops so deliciously clean; all the goods were spread on snow-white cloths, and cloths of similar whiteness were stretched out behind the large hunks of meat hanging up; no blood anywhere, no dirt; the shop-walls and doors were all spruce, balance and weights brightly polished.' She was not aware of the unhygienic slaughter-houses. Until 1845, when London's live cattle market was established in Copenhagen Fields, Islington, animals were driven through the inner London streets to Smithfield, and from there to adjacent slaughter-houses conducted with squalid brutality. Newport Market, near Leicester Square, was another important meat market, with at one time some forty to fifty butchers' shops in the vicinity and several slaughter-houses. Sometimes cattle were casually slaughtered in the yards behind retail butchers' shops – those shops that Sophie found so deliciously clean: 'no blood anywhere, no dirt'.

She was also immensely impressed by the 'brilliant' lighting of London streets, as were other foreign visitors. It was said that when the Prince of Monaco came to London as the guest of George III he arrived in the evening and imagined the street lamps to be a magnificent illumination especially in his honour. But doubtless neither he nor Sophie penetrated into any side streets after dark. These were totally unlit, and prosperous looking pedestrians were liable to be set upon by gangs springing out from hidden alley-ways. You could hire a link-boy to walk in front of you holding up a flaming pitch torch and so avoid the worst of the mire and potholes; but a link-boy was no protection against attack by robbers. There were no policemen until Robert Peel's metropolitan force was formed in 1829, and watchmen were few and far between, often too old and frail to do more than twirl their rattle.

Resident Londoners took a more gloomy view than foreigners of the main street lighting. The Rev. J. Richardson described the parish lamps, as street lamps were called, in his recollections of London at the beginning of the nineteenth century: 'A small tin vessel, half-filled with

the worst train oil [crude whale or fish oil] that the parochial authorities could purchase at the lowest price to themselves and the highest charge to the ratepayers. The lit vessel and wick were enclosed in a case of semi-opaque glass, resembling in shape what Grose, the antiquary, has called the "Night urn of Venus", which being of the very coarsest of vitreous manufacture, obscured even the little light which it encircled.' The more prosperous shopkeepers, however, had 'patent lamps' trained on their windows from outside which, Peller Malcolm wrote, were of infinite service to all pedestrians. They were so bright that 'the parish lamps glimmer above them, and are hardly distinguishable before ten o'clock'. This implies that ten o'clock was the time the shops closed, putting up their shutters.

The first London street to be lit by gas was Pall Mall in 1807. Westminster Bridge was gas-lit by 1813. William Murdoch of Birmingham is generally credited as the inventor, in 1792, of a practical system of lighting by coal-gas; but it was Frederick Albert Winsor who illuminated the south side of Pall Mall with thirteen lamps, the gas being supplied from the 'carbonizing iron furnaces' in Winsor's own house nearby. The illumination was acclaimed a dazzling success, so he straightway formed a National Light and Heat Company, which within a few years was incorporated by Royal Charter as the Gas Light & Coke Company. By the time Miss Weeton arrived in London on the Liverpool coach in May 1824 virtually all the main streets were gas-lit. She wrote: 'Most of the streets are spacious, in excellent repair, and so well lighted by lamps, to a considerable distance, that foreigners arriving by night might have imagined there was universal illumination'. But it was still only the main streets – 'the entering streets are many of them mean, and calculated to inspire foreigners with very erroneous ideas concerning the real magnificence of this metropolis.'

The lamp-man (left) lit oil-burning lamps at sunset in central London. Rowlandson indicated the mixed reactions to the arrival of gas lighting in Pall Mall – no longer 'a dark corner to be got for love or money'.

7 Bond Street and Pall Mall

John Brindley,
BOOKSELLER and STATIONER
at the Kings Arms in New Bond Street,
Bookbinder to Her Majesty and
His Royal Highness the Prince of Wales;

SELLS Books in all Languages, Variety of
Novels, Plays &c.
Also, all Sorts of Stationary Wares, Stampt
Paper, Bonds, Cards, Shop & Pocket Books, &c.
Wholesale and Retail.
Likewise neatly Binds Books in all Sorts of Binding.
Money for any Library or Parcel of Books.

John Brindley, bookseller and stationer, opened the first shop in New Bond Street in 1728 after being a bookbinder in the City. Opposite: *Jane Taylor proved that women, no less than men, could run shops popular with Society.*

BY THE END of the eighteenth century, London had changed its shape. A century previously the built-up area followed a narrow banana shape from Wapping to Westminster, bounded on the south by the Thames and on the north by Holborn and the Oxford Road. By 1800 the shape was roughly square, as a result of the Bloomsbury and Camden developments north of Holborn and the Portman and Harley-Cavendish estates north of Oxford Street. The northern boundary of the metropolis was now the New Road from Paddington to the City. Edgware Road, Park Lane and Grosvenor Place made the western boundary, with tollgates at Tyburn and Hyde Park Corner.

Certain quarters had changed their character. Covent Garden, for example, had acquired an unsavoury reputation. The clientele of its bagnios, or 'sweating houses' – the equivalent of Turkish baths – had become less select; the number of taverns with upper-floors divided into useful cubicles was increasing; out-and-out bawdy houses made no secret of their trade. There were still some good shops and respectable coffee houses, such as Tom's Coffee House, run by Richard Haynes, or Haines, where in the mid-eighteenth century Mr Butcher, the Duke of Bedford's steward, used to have meetings with the Duke's tradesmen and tenants, conducting business in a sociable atmosphere. But there was also the Rose Tavern in Russell Street, which was one of the scenes in Hogarth's *Rake's Progress*; and Tom King's, not to be confused with Tom's Coffee House, founded by the old-Etonian husband of a celebrated procuress. Its main room was decorated with a vast obscene mural of a nun and a monk. Tom King's did not open until midnight and closed at dawn. And dawn brought no peace to the residents of the quarter, since by then waggons and barrows were being trundled into the market, with attendant shouting and swearing. The market itself was increasing every year and overflowing into surrounding streets. One way and another, Covent Garden was not an elegant address. The beau monde had long since pulled out, moving to Leicester Square, to Soho, to the spacious squares of Mayfair – where Hanover Square was the first to be completed in 1719, followed by Grosvenor Square in 1725.

Bond Street was known by the end of the century for its hotels and apartments for gentlemen. The Clarendon Hotel, famed for its

ICH DIEN

Jane Taylor & Son
China and Glass Sellers
to his Royal Highneſs ẏ Prince of Wales,
At the Feathers in Pall Mall,
London.
Sell all Sorts of China Ware, Cutt and
Plain Glaſs, Finest Teas & Chocolate
Wholeſale & Retail.

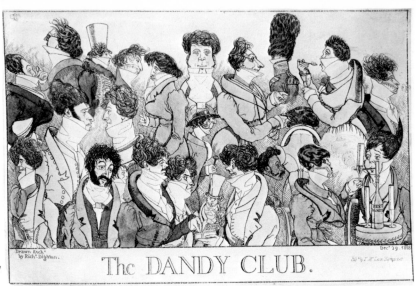

The DANDY CLUB.

Drawn Etch'd
by Richd Dighton.

Decr 29 1818

Members of the Dandy Club
had perforce to devote such
energies as they had to
fashionable shopping: Richard
Dighton's etching of 1818.

outrageously expensive dinners, was run by Monsieur Jacquier, who
had been chef to Louis XVIII. It was in the narrow part of the street
known as the Bond Street Straits, where Cartier the jeweller was later
established – and Asprey's, whose reputation was founded upon fitted
dressing-cases made in its own workrooms above the shop. The
Clarendon ran right through to Albemarle Street, where the carriages
drew up to avoid traffic congestion in 'The Straits'. Stephen's Hotel,
according to Captain Gronow's *Reminiscences*, 'was supported by officers
of the army and men about town. If a stranger asked to dine there, he was
stared at by the servants, and very solemnly assured that there was no
table vacant. It was not an uncommon thing to see thirty or forty saddle
horses and tilburies waiting outside this hotel.' Long's Hotel, at the
Bond Street end of Clifford Street, was originally a coaching-house and
was much patronized by country gentry, who put up there if they came
to London out of season when their town houses were closed. Sir Walter
Scott lived at Long's for some time, and Byron dined with him there.
For arrivals by mail coach there was the Black Horse hostelry, whose
yard entrance arches now mark the salerooms of Sotheby's. The inn's
labyrinthine wine cellars are used as Sotheby's storerooms.

John Brindley's bookshop at 29 New Bond Street was the first shop to
open in the street, in 1728. Brindley had been a well-known City
bookbinder, and his could scarcely be regarded as a retail shop since his
chief business was dealing in antique books and publishing scholarly
works under his own imprint. The first book he published, dedicated to
Queen Caroline, was *Observations on Smallpox* by Dr Richard Holland,
MD, Fellow of the Royal Society – a very topical work, since smallpox,
deadly or at least disfiguring, was then the dreaded scourge of all classes,
rich and poor. It was not until the beginning of the nineteenth century
that Bond Street became known for fashion shops, and then only shops
for men. Beau Brummell and the Prince of Wales, conspicuous style-

Beau Brummell (left) and Bulwer Lytton (right) set standards of sublime dandy brilliance.

setters for the younger generation, considered St James's Street to belong to the fuddy-duddies of the old guard, and led the advance to Bond Street. 'The execution of his [Brummell's] sublime imagination', Captain Gronow noted, 'was carried out by that superior genius, Mr Weston, tailor, of Old Bond Street'. Mitchell's, booksellers and stationers, became a meeting-place for Regency bucks. Count d'Orsay bought all his drawing materials there, and the shop supplied him with his freshly perfumed visiting cards. The dilettante dandies and 'exclusives' who frequented the street naturally attracted tailors, barbers, perfumers, wig-makers and hatters to open shops for them, and some of the shopkeepers themselves became arbiters of fashion. Robert Southey wrote:

There is a professor in the famous Bond-street who, in lessons at half-a-guinea, instructs gentlemen in the art of tying their neck-handkerchiefs in the newest and most approved style. . . . I asked my tailor one day, who is a sensible man in his way, who invented the fashions. 'Why, sir!' said he, 'I believe it is the young gentlemen who walk in Bond-street. They come to me, and give me orders for a new cut, and perhaps it takes, and perhaps it does not. It is all fancy, you know, sir.' It is of as much importance to man as to woman, that he should appear in the prevailing colour. My tailor tells me I must have pantaloons of a reddish cast, 'All on the reds now, sir' . . . and reddish accordingly they are, in due conformity to his prescription.

Thackeray's ageing but indomitable beau, Major Pendennis, is described as coming out of his dressing-room 'neat and radiant, and preceded by faint odours from Delcroix's shop, from which emporium Major Pendennis's wig and his pocket handkerchief got their perfume.' The wig itself was a creation of the celebrated Mr Truefitt of Old Bond Street: 'A little gray had been introduced into the coiffure of late by Mr. Truefitt, which had given the Major's head the most artless and respectable appearance.' Later, when Bond Street was beginning to be infiltrated by furriers, milliners and court dressmakers, Truefitt & Hill opened the first ladies' hairdressing salon in the street. Having no plumbing, they installed built-in marble shampooing basins, with plugged outlets and a slop-pail beneath. The assistants were like ladies' maids, dressed in black with white caps. When they opened a manicure court – all potted palms and gilt-framed mirrors – they imported a manicurist from America. Truefitt's recipe for lip salve was guaranteed, if correctly followed, to 'last two years without losing its colour'. The colouring ingredient was cochineal.

Major Pendennis's tailor was not Beau Brummell's Mr Weston, but the equally famous Stultz, established from 1809 at 10 Clifford Street, off Bond Street. The dandy hero of Bulwer Lytton's *Pelham* set a fashion both in literature and life by wearing black evening clothes and insisting that Stultz make his suits without padding. Stultz also crops up in many nineteenth-century memoirs, including the libellous reminiscences of the famous courtesan Harriette Wilson. She relates that a masquerade was being given by the members of Wattier's Club in honour of the peace between Britain and France, and she

accompanied Julie to Mr Stultz, the German regimental tailor and moneylender in Clifford Street. We asked Stultz's advice about a modest disguise for Julie, and he referred us to a book full of drawings therein exhibited, the dress of an Italian or Austrian peasant-boy or girl, I forget which. Stultz brought home our dresses himself in his tilbury, on the morning of the masquerade, being anxious that we should do him credit. Everything fitted us to a hair.

Stultz had out-of-town clients, including ladies – among them Sara Hutchinson. She wrote from Brinsop Court, Herefordshire, on 20 April 1829, to Edward Quillian in London, asking him to call on Stultz to order her a new riding habit.

Chuse the cloth, *good, stout* and *dark* blue, pay for it and send me the amount of the *damage* and I will return the money by post . . . order him to send the habit by the Mail to Hereford to be left at the Greyhound for Mr. H., Brinsop Court – and be sure to be sent as soon as possible – I wish to pay for it immediately that I may have a discount.

It is interesting to learn from this letter that Stultz gave a discount for cash – a concession that women were more likely to take advantage of than men about town. At Lock's the hatters, any customer who preferred to settle immediately made a deduction of a shilling in the pound – this was understood and not actually mentioned. But very few of Lock's clients were cash customers. Hatters and tailors were accustomed to giving long credit, and the more aristocratic the customer the longer the account was allowed to remain unpaid – three to four years was quite usual. Harriette Wilson, in calling Stultz a moneylender, may only have meant it in the sense that he gave his clients indefinite credit.

Lord Byron, when a schoolboy at Harrow, had his clothes made by his father's tailor, James Milne of Grosvenor Street. Milne had in 1786 bailed Captain Jack Byron out of the King's Bench prison, where he had been imprisoned for debt to the amount of £176 – so there was a certain

Fribourg & Treyer, whose shop in the Haymarket remains the same after two and a half centuries.

obligation for his son to remain loyal to Milne. As Mrs Byron was paying the bills at that time, Milne probably did have his settled. When she died, Lord Byron had to furnish his staff at Knebworth with mourning clothes, and the Nottingham tailors were still asking for a remittance three years later. At the same time, another bill for servant's clothes of £174 19s 6d was running with Thomas Edwards at 52 Conduit Street, off Bond Street.

Bond Street, with its hotels and apartments, its tailors, wig-makers, and bookshops, its bucks and its beaux, was in Regency times very much a man's street – after dark a prostitute beat. But Pall Mall had changed its character by the end of the eighteenth century. The masculine atmosphere of coffee houses and clubs was no longer dominant, and it had become a fashionable shopping street for ladies as well as men. Jane Taylor & Son, 'China and Glass Sellers to His Royal Highness ye Prince of Wales', was at the Feathers, Pall Mall, selling 'all sorts of China ware, Cutt and Plain Glass'. Like most china shops, it also sold 'finest Tea and Chocolate, wholesale and retail'. At the Haymarket end of Pall Mall there was the goldsmith's shop of William and Mary Deards at The Star.

There were two bookshops, probably the earliest established being that of Jackson, who is mentioned in *The Oldest London Bookshop* as having been a distributor, in 1727, of a book bound by John Brindley before Brindley himself started his bookshop in New Bond Street. The other Pall Mall bookshop was that of Robert Dodsley at the Tully's Head, which opened in 1735 and became a gathering place for literary people. Then there was James Fribourg, snuff dealer, at the Rasp and Crown, the rasp being the principal tool of the snuff-makers' trade. In 1720, the Rasp and Crown, by then under the management of Fribourg & Treyer, moved from Pall Mall to No. 34 'at the Upper End of ye Haymarket' – where Fribourg & Treyer still are, still selling snuff, still in the same little shop with its eighteenth-century windows. Another interesting partnership was that of Mouys & Jarritt, hatters, who provided a hat rental service. They took in old hats in exchange for new and stripped them down for re-manufacture. They also cleaned and repaired customers' hats – as indeed did all the high-class hatters of St James's, provided the hats were *their* hats.

The most handsome private residence in Pall Mall became a retail shop before the eighteenth century was out. This was Schomberg House, which still stands today. It was built in 1698 to plans prepared by Dutch architects for the 2nd Duke of Schomberg, who came to England with William III. Subsequent owners included the Duke of Cumberland, and when he died in 1765 the house was bought by the artist John Astley, who divided the interior into three dwellings without altering the beautiful frontage on Pall Mall. Astley occupied the centre house, and tenants of the other two included the artists Richard Cosway and Thomas Gainsborough, who had his home and studio in the west wing from 1774 until his death in 1788.

Schomberg House in Pall Mall, c. 1850.

*Harding, Howell & Co.,
stylish occupants of Schomberg
House from 1796 to 1820.*

In 1781 the east wing was taken by Dr James Graham for his Temple of Hymen and Health, moved from the Adelphi. Dr Graham was a quack doctor specializing in sex problems, with theories about electrical treatment. For a night in the 'Celestial Bed', guaranteed to cure sterility, £50 was the usual charge. Lectures were given on subjects such as 'The Causes, Nature and Effects of Love and Beauty at the different Periods of Human Life in Persons and Personages, Male, Female, and Demi-Characters'. During the lectures, tableaux were staged of diaphanously draped 'goddesses of Health and Beauty', one of whom was the fifteen-year-old Emily Hart, who changed her name to Emma and years later, after many vicissitudes, became Lady Hamilton.

It is unlikely that Gainsborough and his aristocratic friends and patrons thought the next tenants of the east wing, Messrs Dyde & Scribe, much improvement on Dr Graham, since they turned it into a retail shop. But their merchandise was akin to art. Their pencilled furniture calicoes and glazed chintzes, produced by the then recent invention of roller printing, carried designs by the most talented English and Continental fabric designers. The designs were so beautiful that they quickly became the height of furnishing fashion, and the presence in Pall Mall of the leading impresarios of this art form brought other fabric specialists to the street: at No. 61, Abraham Allen sold chintzes of his own design; at No. 49, Harris, Muddy & Co. sold 'copper-plate cotton furnishings for lounge, drawing-room, boudoir and sleeping'. Pall Mall became *the* shopping street for soft furnishings.

It was in 1784 that Dyde and Scribe came to Pall Mall, and by 1796 they had made enough money to retire in luxury. They sold their business to Harding, Howell & Co., who at the same time acquired the other two sections of Schomberg House and created London's first department store. The ground floor was redesigned into five departments – or shops as they called them – separated by glazed mahogany partitions. An illustration in Ackermann's *Repository of the Arts* for 1809 shows this interior in all its spacious dignity, and the accompanying article describes the disposition of the merchandise. Immediately at the entrance was the 'shop' for furs and fans. The next shop contained 'articles of haberdashery of every description, silks, muslins, lace, gloves, etc.' To the right 'you meet with a rich assortment of jewellery, ornamental articles in ormolu, French clocks, and so on, and on the left, with all the different kinds of perfumery necessary for the toilette.' Another department sold millinery and dresses, and 'there is no article of female attire or decoration but what may be procured in the first style of elegance and fashion'. Small furniture was displayed on the ground floor of the west wing, while the east wing held 'every article of foreign manufacture which there is any possibility of obtaining'. The fine original staircase of the Duke's mansion led up to a room with a wide view over St James's Park to Westminster and the Surrey hills beyond. During Richard Cosway's tenancy it had been his breakfast room, and it was still known as Mr Cosway's breakfast room. Here customers were served with wines, tea, coffee and sweetmeats, and it made a charming rendezvous. The entire selling space on this restaurant floor was devoted to the display of furnishing fabrics, the firm's great speciality; and on the floor above were the workrooms: 'Forty persons are regularly employed on the premises in making up the various articles offered for sale, and in attendance on the different departments.'

The firm enjoyed royal patronage. St James's Palace was just up the road, and Schomberg House backed upon Marlborough House with a communicating door in the party-wall. George III commissioned the design and printing of hangings for his bedroom at Kew Palace, and he marketed through Harding, Howell & Co. the Anglo-merino cloth woven from fleeces of the royal merino flock at Windsor Park, cloth described as 'nearly as fine as muslin in its texture and highly elegant for evening wear . . . the closest imitation to the real Indian shawl fabric ever produced in this country.' Dress silks woven at Spitalfields were also designed exclusively for Queen Charlotte and the princesses; and the firm was granted permission to sell certain patterns under the name of Queen's Silk. When the Prince of Wales ordered hangings to be designed for his bedroom at Carlton House, the firm was permitted to market 'this rich furniture chintz'. To advertise it, a cutting was pasted into each copy of an 1811 issue of Ackermann's *Repository of the Arts*.

When steam-driven machine printing was introduced, chintz prices

The chintzes used for the Prince of Wales's bedroom furnishings at Carlton House, 1811: actual patterns pasted into Ackermann's Repository.

The Repository

Of Arts, Literature, Commerce, Manufactures, Fashions, and Politics.

MANUFACTURERS, Factors, and Wholesale Dealers in Fancy Goods, that come within the scope of this Plan, are requested to send Patterns of such new Articles, as they come out; and if the requisites of Novelty, Fashion, and Elegance, are united, the quantity necessary for this Magazine will be ordered.

R. Ackermann, 101, *Strand, London.*

fell. Available to a much wider public, they lost their exclusive appeal, and Harding, Howell & Co. do not seem to have lowered their sights to the middle-class market – after all, Pall Mall was *not* a middle-class street. Their luxury trade in other goods also fell off, because the Napoleonic Wars cut off supplies from the Continent and caused a general trade depression. Two new partners were taken, the firm becoming Harding, Howell, Ashby & James, but the decline was not arrested; and in 1820 Howell and James split away, setting up their own business at Nos. 5, 7 and 9 Regent Street, which became one of the most fashionable shops throughout the nineteenth century. The old firm continued at Schomberg House as Harding, Ashby, Allsop & Co. into the 1830s, by which time most of the other Pall Mall shops had disappeared. Nash's new building for the United Services Club had set the pattern for what soon became a dull street of dignified gentlemen's clubs designed in the Italianate palazzo style. Alone of the seventeenth-century buildings, Schomberg House remained, but as accommodation for the War Office. It is now occupied by an insurance company.

In the first decades of the nineteenth century, there was one redoubtable woman shopkeeper in the masculine stronghold of St James's. This was Mrs Bell, wife of John Bell the publisher, bookseller and owner of Bell's Circulating Library. In 1820 Mrs Bell achieved sartorial fame for her invention of the *Chapeau Bras*, an ingenious type of calash, or hooped hood, which folded up for carrying in a lady's 'ridicule', as Regency handbags were called. Her first shop was at 22 Upper King Street, Covent Garden; then, prospering, she moved to 26 Charlotte Street. Some time before 1830 she moved again to No. 3 Cleveland Row, opposite St James's Palace – no higher could she move! There she opened her *Magazin de Modes* with 'a novel and splendid display of Millinery, Dresses, and Head-dresses, just prepared in Paris exclusively for Mrs. Bell'. She employed French, German and Spanish milliners and dressmakers, and had 'agents in every foreign country to provide her *exclusively* twice each week with every foreign novelty'. Ladies' dresses, riding habits, fancy ball dresses, wedding dresses and family mourning did not exhaust Mrs Bell's designing talents. She was a corset inventress, holding the appointment of 'Corset Maker to Her Royal Highness the Duchess of Kent', which means it is very likely she had the honour, or onus, of making the corsets which cradled, so to speak, the embryo Queen Victoria. Mrs Bell's 'Bandage Corset' was invented for use before and after accouchement, and also for ladies inclined to corpulency – which seems to cover the demands of the Duchess of Kent both in and out of pregnancy. Mrs Bell's 'Regenerating and Sleeping Ceinture' was also indispensable to ladies before and after accouchement ('prevents flatulency, reduces protuberance, supports the stomach and bowels, relieves dropsical symptoms').

Furthermore, Mrs Bell was, from 1824, the director of an elegant monthly published by her husband, named *The World of Fashion and*

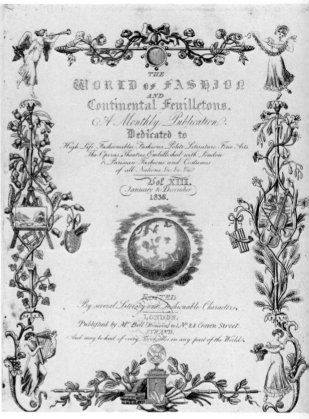

Continental Feuilletons. It was 'dedicated expressly to High Life, Fashionables and Fashions, Polite Literature, Fine Arts, The Opera, Theatres, etc.', and had gossip columns under the headings of 'High Life and Fashionable Chit Chat', and 'On-Dits of Fashion'. Naturally it carried a great deal of advertising for Mrs Bell's shop, disguised as editorial. The issues for 1830 and 1831 trod a tricky course between writing up Mrs Bell's direct connection with French fashions, and espousing a 'Buy British' campaign led by Queen Adelaide to aid the silk-weavers of Spitalfields, English manufacturers of woollen cloth, and workers in the fashion trades. The issue of 1 March 1831 carried the pleasing headline 'French Blondes on the Decline', blonde being a species of lace. In the same issue Queen Adelaide herself was accused of hypocrisy in her 'Buy British' campaign. A long letter to the Editor from 'An Englishwoman' alleged that 'a considerable number of Her Majesty's appointments have been conferred upon *foreigners* ... the dresses which decorate (*or are meant to decorate*) the *Queenly form*, are the work of the people of one *Madame X* (I dare say she is a *volume* of vanity if one knew all)' and that 'the *perruquier* of the palace, and the pavilion, figures and fidgets away in the fantastical person of Monsieur P.'

Formal dress for different occasions, published in John Bell's La Belle Assemblée, 1830 (left). His magazine The World of Fashion *provided valuable publicity, disguised as editorial, for his wife's shop.*

8 Shopping by mail coach – Society and shopkeepers

THE CHARACTER of Piccadilly changed with the introduction of regular mail coaches in 1784. Several Piccadilly inns acted as termini for the West Country coaches, and the Portsmouth mail set out from the Gloster Coffee House. It seems from *Vanity Fair* that this coffee house had overnight accommodation: Mrs Bute Crawley was going to take a vacant room there when she arrived by the Portsmouth coach, though in the event Miss Crawley invited her to stay in her Park Lane house.

At No. 75 Piccadilly, the Three Kings was the terminus for the first Bath coach. The Bull and Mouth, where Swan & Edgar is now, served the Shropshire mails. On the south side of Piccadilly, there was the Lemon Tree on the corner of the Haymarket, and the White Bear Inn, each of them with a coach office and stabling for over forty horses. Further west along Piccadilly, there was the White Horse Cellar (later Hatchett's Restaurant) at the corner of Dover Street. It was from the coach office of the White Horse Cellar that Lock's dispatched their hats to customers in the West Country. For example, one entry in Lock's books noted the dispatch for Mr William Pitt of 'a light Thanet with square crown, silk binding and band' to Somerton in Somerset, consigned in a wooden box to 'the book-keeper at the White Horse Cellar for onward transmission by stage coach'. One of Lock's West Country customers used to 'prestall his bills' by sending hampers of turkeys, salmon, mutton or brawn to the White Horse Cellar for the Lock household.

Mail transport was speedy, and private citizens sending parcels worried if they did not hear of their parcel's arrival within the week. Charles Lamb wrote to William Hazlitt on 15 March 1806: 'I am a little surprised at no letter from you. This day week, to wit Saturday the 8th March 1806, I book'd off by the Wem Coach, Bull and Mouth Inn, directed to *you* at the Revd. Mr Hazlitt's, Wem, Shropshire, a parcel containing besides a book etc. a rare print which I take to be a Titian; begging the said W. H. to acknowledge receipt thereof; which he not having done, I conclude the said parcel to be lying at the Inn and may be lost.' Sara Hutchinson commissioned her cousin John Monkhouse 'to purchase for me at your friend the Chip Hat house a Chip Hat or Bonnet of the very *newest* fashion', giving him the most detailed description of

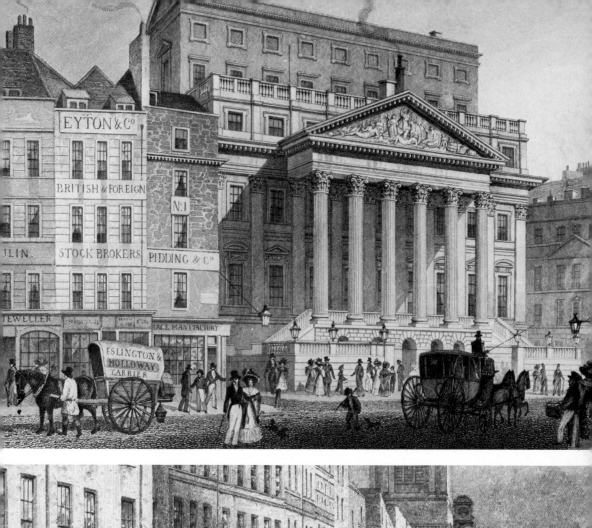

*The Bull & Mouth, on the
site of Swan & Edgar in
Piccadilly. The Duke of
Beaufort coach, seen here,
aimed to reach Brighton in four
and a half hours.*

what she wanted. This order took a maddeningly long time. Sara kept writing to John about it, her last letter ending: 'I will therefore trouble you once more to enquire what coach it was sent by, to what Inn at York and the Innkeeper's name'; then a petulant postscript: 'But as it is too late in the season it is of little consequence – you need not trouble yourself.' We know exactly how Sara felt.

Quite often country families who rarely came to London appointed the proprietor of a London coaching inn to act as their agent for shopping and other business. The Purefoy family of Shalstone in Buckinghamshire, some sixty miles from London, chose Thomas Robotham, proprietor of the King's Head in Islington. He had married a former maid of the Purefoys, so was known to them personally. They also appointed Peter Moulson, a City wine merchant, as another agent. These two men acted as intermediaries between the Purefoys and London tradesmen, conducted business connected with property they owned in the capital and even advised on investment matters.

Mrs Purefoy requested Mr Robotham to do quite personal shopping for her, as on 14 July 1736: 'Pray get me 4 dozen yards of lace the same to the pattern; if you can't have it ready made, there is a man keeps a little lace shop over against St. Clement's Church on the side next the Thames. He will make it at two and twenty pence or two shillings the dozen yards.' In another letter she asked for information on the latest fashions: 'I desire Mrs Robotham will send me a pattern of the newest fashioned dressed night clothes and ruffles and a pattern of the newest fashioned mobb.' Her son Henry Purefoy also liked to keep up with the London fashions, writing on 4 August 1744: 'I desire you will send me 5 yards of silver lace to bind a waistcoat as good and fashionable as any is worn – as also two dozen and four silver twist buttons for the waistcoat. . . . Send these by the Buckingham carrier . . . send your bill with them and [I] will order you payment.' In country towns it was usual for bookselling to be a sideline of some tradesman who undertook to order books from London publishers – it could be the draper, the ironmonger, any shopkeeper. It was through the baker at Brackley that the Purefoys bought their books.

Families who had no London agent relied upon county carriers, whose waggons went on regular days from all the larger provincial towns to appointed London inns. The carrier's waggon was less expensive because less speedy than the mail coach. Charles Lamb wrote to William Wordsworth: 'I have seen the books which you ordered booked at the White Horse Inn Cripplegate by the Kendal Waggon this day, 1st Feb. 1806.' And to Dorothy Wordsworth:

I have booked this 2nd June 1804 from The Waggon Inn, Cripplegate, the watch and books which I got from your brother Richard, together with Purchas's *Pilgrimage* and Browne's *Religio Medici* . . . with some pens, of which I observed no great frequency when I tarried at Grasmere. These things I have put up in a deal box directed to Mr. Wordsworth, Grasmere, near Ambleside, Kendal, by the *Kendal* waggon. At the same time I have sent off a parcel by Charles's desire to Mr. T. Hutchinson . . . by the Penrith waggon this day; which I beg you to apprize them of, lest my direction fail. . . . In your box, you will find a little parcel for Mrs. Coleridge, which she wants as soon as possible; also for yourselves, the Cotton, Magnesia, Bark and Oil, which came to £2.3.4.

We learn from William H. Ablett's *Reminiscences of an Old Draper* that, before the railway era, City wholesalers in the drapery trade delivered goods to their shopkeeper customers as far away as Wales by four-horse waggon: 'They used to start on their long journey with as much punctuality as the coaches did.' Many provincial shopkeepers came themselves by mail coach to London to select the latest merchandise from City wholesalers. In the early 1780s, Elizabeth Towsey, who with her sister Susannah kept a millinery shop in Chester, travelled to London twice a year to select from the new season's fashions. When their selection arrived at Chester an advertisement in the local paper invited customers to come and inspect them. It was this little shop run by the two sisters which, through Susannah marrying a druggist, Mr Brown, and their son carrying on the millinery business, became the famous Brown's department store of Chester. With the Manchester wholesale drapers so near Chester, it is surprising that the Towseys should have made the long journey to choose their stock from City wholesalers; but the prestige of London fashions – even more of Paris fashions imported into

London – evidently made it worth the expenditure of time and money. Knutsford, also near Manchester, was Mrs Gaskell's *Cranford*; and she makes the principal shopkeeper, 'who ranged from grocer, to cheesemonger, to man-milliner', claim that he went straight to London for the fashions which he exhibited at the beginning of each season in his rooms in the High Street. Millinery did not mean just hats, as in modern times, but embraced all ladies' wear and fashion accessories. As R. Campbell put it: 'Milliners furnish Everything to the Ladies that can contribute to set off their Beauty, increase their Vanity, or render them ridiculous.'

London newspapers were sent to the provinces through the Post Office by the night mail coaches. This meant they were already twelve hours old before starting on their long journeys. So William Henry Smith and his brother, whose business as 'Stationers and Newsmen' at 42 Duke Street and 192 Strand was started by their father at 4 Little Grosvenor Street in 1792, resolved to by-pass the Post Office. They organized carts to collect the newspapers as they came off the presses in the early hours of the morning, and to deliver them to the *morning* mail coaches, which were faster than the night mails as well as starting half a day earlier. If the mail coach had left the terminus before Smith's cart got there, the driver would pursue it hell-for-leather and transfer the bundles of papers wherever the coach was overtaken.

When there was news of great national interest, Smith's drivers were instructed to disregard the coaches altogether. They obtained relays of horses *en route*, and themselves delivered the papers to the main provincial cities. On the day George IV died, Smith's chartered a boat and delivered the newspapers to Dublin a full twenty-four hours ahead of even the Royal Messenger. When the railways came, Smith's took over nine express engines for their newspaper traffic. They delivered papers in Edinburgh an hour and a half, and in Glasgow two hours, before the mails which left London the previous evening. In 1848 the first W. H. Smith railway bookstall was opened at Euston, and it was from these bookstalls that they began a library service in 1858. The W. H. Smith high-street shops did not start until 1906.

Passenger coach fares became very competitive on the relatively short routes. Mrs Fitzherbert wrote to Thomas Creevey from Brighton in 1818, deploring the cheap coaches that were bringing the *hoi polloi* to that elegant royal watering-place: 'I cannot boast of much good society which formerly we abounded with at this season. When I tell you that fifty-two public coaches go from hence to London every day and bring people down for six shillings, you will not be surprised at the sort of company we have.' On the long-distance routes fares were standardized, as Miss Weeton found when she enquired about the fares to Liverpool at all the coach offices in Piccadilly and Oxford Street. Everywhere it was £4 travelling inside, £2 outside. Miss Weeton, who had to count every penny, travelled outside, setting off from the Spread Eagle, Piccadilly, at 5.45 in the morning.

The shops near the Piccadilly coach offices were naturally of the kind to supply the immediate needs of travellers and to attract tourists. Miss

Loading for express delivery of
The Times *by W. H. Smith*
*in 1859 (*left*). The station*
bookstall became a familiar
feature from the mid-nineteenth
*century onwards (*below*).*

Weeton described a shop window where 'disposed amongst the drapery, were cards written in a large Roman hand. . . . Napoleons sold and bought. Light guineas taken at full value. Old silver taken with rapture. French silver taken with alacrity, quite novel. Napoleons, Louis d'ors and Gold of every sort and denomination taken with peculiar adroitness.' 'Light guineas' were chipped or otherwise mutilated coins, which few shopkeepers were prepared to accept. No new silver was struck for most of the eighteenth century, so that coins were wearing thin, and were in any case insufficient for the increase in the spending population. Shilling and sixpenny pieces became so thin that some shopkeepers weighed them on their scales and demanded that the customer make up the proper weight of silver.

Across the road from this shop, at No. 10 Piccadilly next to the Bull and Mouth, Swan & Edgar had been established in 1812. William Edgar was the son of a Cumberland farmer, and started his London career by selling men's haberdashery on a market stall. One version of how and where he met George Swan is that Swan had a nearby stall in the same market. Another has it that Swan was already established in a profitable business in the city. There was, in fact, a Mr Swan at 10 Fore Street in the City, to whom the first of the Debenhams was apprenticed in the very early nineteenth century. This Mr Swan could well have been the father, or uncle, of George Swan who, having learned his trade in the family shop, might have decided to start on his own in the West End. Unfortunately, the only recorded fact is that George Swan died without issue in 1821. What a bizarre quirk of fate that the name of this Swan, whose only known years as a shopkeeper amounted to nine, should still be written large in Piccadilly Circus, familiar to generations of visitors to London from all over the world. In contrast, William Edgar's life is well documented. He flourished both financially and socially; one of his three daughters achieved marriage with a baronet, Sir Henry Peak. One of his three sons followed him into the business and had eleven children, just one of whom deigned to go into the family firm.

Thirteen years before Miss Weeton's solitary visit to London, another provincial lady from a different social stratum was writing letters from London. Jane Austen stayed with her brother Henry at No. 64 Sloane Street in April 1811, a few months before the publication of *Sense and Sensibility*. She wrote to her sister Cassandra of taking a walk to Grafton House; 'and I am sorry to tell you that I am getting very extravagant and spending all my Money'. Grafton House was at No. 164 New Bond Street, on the corner of Grafton Street, at that time owned by the drapers Wilding & Kent and later by the Grafton Fur Company. It was evidently a popular shop, because the Austens 'set off immediately after Breakfast and must have reached Grafton House by $\frac{1}{2}$ past 11 – , but when we entered the Shop, the whole Counter was thronged, and we waited *full* half an Hour before we could be attended to.' On another visit to her brother, when he had moved after his wife's death into rooms over the bank of which he was a partner in Henrietta Street, Covent Garden, she wrote to Cassandra: 'At nine we are to set off for Grafton House, and get that over before Breakfast.' By going early 'we got immediate

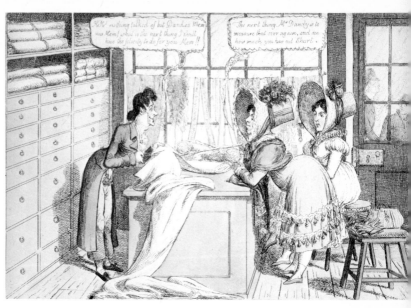

Attendance and went on very comfortably'. Layton & Shear of Bedford House, being near Henrietta Street, was conveniently placed for before-breakfast visits: 'Very pretty English poplins at 4.3d; Irish, ditto at 6s; *more* than pretty, certainly – beautiful.' Jane visited Christian's of Wigmore Street to buy her niece Fanny's dimity; and Fanny herself 'bought her Irish at Newton's in Leicester Square'. In March 1814, Jane reported to Cassandra that she had seen 'a great many pretty Caps in the Windows of Cranbourn Alley!' Her exclamation mark may have been because Cranbourn Alley, well known for its cheap bonnet shops, had a doubtful reputation owing to its proximity to Seven Dials, notorious haunt of prostitutes.

Jane Austen's letters, full of prices and details of purchases, were not written for publication. Very different were the *Letters from England* of her contemporary Robert Southey, published anonymously in 1807 and purporting to be translated from the Spanish of 'Don Manuel Alvarez Espriella'. Allowing for a good pinch of poetic salt, the letters show that the City was still holding its own as a shopping centre. Southey wrote of the carriages and crowds in Cheapside, and was

astonished at the opulence and splendour of the shops; drapers, stationers, confectioners, pastry-cooks, seal-cutters, silver-smiths, book-sellers, print-sellers, hosiers, fruiterers, china-sellers – one close to another, without intermission, a shop to every house, street after street, and mile after mile. . . . The finest gentlemen to be seen in the streets of London are the men who serve at the linen-drapers and mercers. Early in the morning they are drest *cap-à-pied*, the hair feathered and frosted with a delicacy which no hat is to derange through the day. They are to be seen after breakfast at their respective shop-doors, paring their nails, and adjusting their cravats. . . . Luxury here fills every head with caprice, from the servant-maid to the peeress, and shops are become exhibitions of fashion. In the spring, when all persons of distinction are in Town, the usual morning employment of the ladies is to go a-shopping, as it is called. This they do without actually wanting to purchase anything, and they spend their money or not, according to the temptations which are held out to gratify and amuse.

As in Fanny Burney's *Evelina* twenty-five years earlier, surprise is expressed that the assistants were always men: 'So many young men are employed in London to recommend muslins to the ladies, to assist them in the choice of a gown, to weigh out thread and to measure ribbons . . . but female shopkeepers, it is said, have not enough patience to indulge this idle and fastidious curiosity; whereas young men are more assiduous, more engaging, and not at all querulous about their loss of time.' Although so rapturous about the splendour of City shops, Southey allows that 'at the West End of the Town, there is some degree of consequence connected with the situation. . . . A transit from the City to the West End of the Town is the last step of the successful trader, when he throws off his *exuvia* and emerges from his chrysalis state into the butterfly world of high life.'

It was not as easy as Southey suggested to throw off the exuviae of retail trade. In following the westward progression of the nobility and gentry, a tradesman might grow rich, might even achieve a title, but his social standing would be down-graded. In the City of London, commerce was the traditional source of wealth, and the men who contributed to that wealth were respected and honoured. As R. Campbell wrote: 'By serving an Apprenticeship of seven years, a Youth becomes Free of this great City, and may hope one Day to be exalted to the Mayorality; since we have many Instances of Men from the lowest Circumstances of Life who have arrived at and filled that Chair with Honour and Reputation.' But honour in the City cut no ice in the West End, where 'birth' was everything and ennobled tradesmen were sneered at as 'City Knights'.

There was a pastry-cook Lord Mayor in 1815. This was Samuel Birch of Birch, Birch & Co. of 15 Cornhill. Founded in the reign of George I as confectioners and suppliers to civic banquets, their great speciality was an annual display of enormous, extremely elaborate Twelfth Night cakes. Their shop was also famous for turtle soup, venison and oyster pies, served in an unpretentious, clean dining-room approached through the kitchen and bakehouse. The Lord Mayor of 1824 was a linen-draper, Sir Robert Waithman, who was member of Parliament for the City of London. It was said that his speeches in the House were usually drowned by deliberate coughs and the muttered conversations of Members who resented a retailer's entry into London's most privileged club. Thomas Creevey wrote to his stepdaughter describing a dinner at the Mansion House.

The Waithman Family, both male and female, were in all their glory. I could not help thinking when I looked at them, what they must think of their *shop*, poor things, when they return to it after all their finery. There were at least 8 or 10 Livery Servants covered with lace, in silk stockings and buckles, to say nothing of my Lord Mayor's State *Postillon* who stood behind his lordship's back all the time, in full costume booted and spurred, and wearing his cap *on*, which evidently must have been made at the silversmith's and mounting at least two

SHERIFF DOUBLE-HUE;
half DEVIL half RADICAL.

*Sir Robert Waithman, Lord Mayor in
1824 and MP for the City of London. A
'mere' linen-draper, he was depicted by
Richard Dighton in 1821 as 'half DEVIL
half RADICAL.'*

feet above his head. My Lord and My lady sat 'jig by jole' (is that right?) occupying the head of the table to their noble selves. The Chaplain at the bottom in full Canonicals – the Duke of Sussex, and at least thirty of us ranged down the sides.

One of the employees at Waithman's shop was the William Ablett who some fifty years later wrote his *Reminiscences of an Old Draper*:

I was the first shawl-man at Robert Waithman's, whose shop used to be at the corner of Fleet-Street and Ludgate-hill. He was a draper dealing in rich damasks, muslins, and shawls principally. In those days there were enormous duties imposed on many kinds of goods; amongst others, India shawls were very heavily weighted in this respect, and ladies coming from India would bring as many with them as could be made to pass muster as their own clothing in use, which they would sell to Waithman who paid great attention to this part of the business.

It must surely have been Waithman that Thackeray intended when he wrote of the widowed Amelia Osborne, desperately in need of money, remembering 'a fine India shop on Ludgate Hill, where the ladies had all sorts of dealings and bargains in shawls'. Amelia packed up the shawl sent to her from India by Major Dobbin and walked all the way from Brompton village to Ludgate Hill. 'She was not mistaken as to the value of the Major's gift. It was a very fine and beautiful silk and the merchant made a very good bargain when he gave her twenty guineas for her shawl.'

In *Pendennis* Thackeray described London when the Season was over and 'the tradesmen of St James's were abroad taking their pleasure; the tailors had grown mustachios and were gone up the Rhine; the bootmakers were at Ems or Baden, blushing when they met their customers at those places of recreation, or punting beside their creditors at the gaming tables'. But not all the tradesmen of St James's were blushingly sensitive about their calling. In *Mr. Lock of St. James's Street*, we learn that the third Mr James Lock was 'even invited by some of his customers to stay in their fine houses. He was always good company and, being a bachelor, was useful for matching numbers at a dinner table. It was far from usual for a tradesman to be invited out of his own circle; but the circle of St James's shopkeepers was a very cultured one, and from it he moved outwards with ease, for he was entirely without social pretension.' When this Mr Lock retired at seventy, he married the twenty-eight year old daughter of John Selot, a partner in Fortnum & Mason's.

Thackeray's contemporary Mrs Gore, of the 'Silver Fork' school of novelists, dissected the snobberies of Society with lethal accuracy in her *Women As They Are*. James Mordaunt, brother of the heroine of the novel, Lady Willersdale, writes to tell her of the engagement of one of their younger sisters:

The young gentleman who has so kindly consented to disencumber my father and mother of their fourth and frightful daugher, is a heavy, good-looking fellow of five-and-twenty; belonging to one of those Scotch merchandizing families who grub their way upwards from some lane in the City, to a

The baker's boy called every day. A drawing by Thackeray.

Baronetage, and a seat in the House. His father is of the description of monied men, whose names perpetually stare at one from the lists of India Directors, Bank Directors, Insurance Offices (capital one million sterling) and subscriptions for Spanish refugees. He lives in Harley Street, drives a phaeton with red wheels, and gives his heir apparent – Jane's infatuated adorer – five thousand a-year.

A little later we are told how Mrs Forsyth, mother of the 'infatuated adorer', had nagged her merchant husband into moving out of the City to Bloomsbury; and then, when the tide of fashion flowed further westwards, she made him move again to Harley Street. Even the Harley Street/Cavendish Square quarter was not the equal of Mayfair. In Mrs Gore's *Mothers and Daughters*, Eleanor Willingham, who has hopes of marrying a duke, says it is unthinkable to ask him to dine with 'men who were never dreampt of on the southern side of Oxford Street'. Another character in the same novel speaks of 'A Sir Westland Somebody – or Sir Somebody Westland; one of our commercial upstarts, as rich as the Bank and as vulgar as Oxford Street'.

Thackeray placed the Sedleys and the Osbornes in Russell Square, Bloomsbury, both fathers being wealthy City merchants; and Miss Crawley's footmen, when she drove with Becky Sharp from her house in Park Lane to call on the Sedleys, 'wondered at the locality in which they found themselves'. Russell Square seems to have been a particular target for sneers as being the preserve of City merchants. *Punch*, in a feature named 'The Geology of Society' (16 October 1841), divided 'High Life' into two classes: the 'Superior Class', called the St James's Series, and the 'Transition Class', which was the Russell Square group. In the latter were 'People who keep a carriage, but are silent respecting their grandfathers; people who give dinners to the superior series of St James's; and people who talk of the four per-cents, and are suspected of being mixed up in a grocery concern in the City.' In *Vanity Fair*, William Dobbins's father 'was an Alderman, and thought to be very rich' – a merchant banker, perhaps. But a dreadful day came at William's school when a cart emblazoned DOBBIN AND RUDGE, GROCERS & OILMEN was seen delivering goods at the tradesmen's entrance.

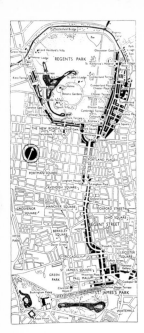

Nash's Regent Street and its immediate surroundings.

9 Nash's Regent Street changes the pattern of shopping

IN JULY 1813, Parliament passed the Act for the building of Regent Street. Instigated by the Prince Regent, planned by John Nash, it was to provide a magnificent carriageway from the Regent's residence at Carlton House to the new royal park which had recently been laid out in Marylebone Park, where the Prince intended to have a villa. From Piccadilly to Portland Place, Regent Street followed the course of an existing street called Swallow Street, a short stretch of which still remains, cutting through from Piccadilly to the south side of the Quadrant. Naturally there were violent objections from owners of the Swallow Street property designated to be demolished, but it seems to have been a street ripe for clearance. It was described by Augustus Sala as having been 'a long, devious, dirty thoroughfare, which three generations since was full of pawnbrokers' dram-shops, and more than equivocal livery stables, which were said to be extensively patronised by professional highwaymen'.

South of Piccadilly, St James's Market was demolished, a new market being constructed between the new street and the Haymarket. Around the market were built small shops such as ironmongers, grocers and chemists; also modest houses for tradesmen serving the district: builders, plumbers, carpenters, house-decorators. A similar 'domestic' area with a market had been laid out at the Marylebone Park end of the majestic new Regent Street, together with two 'model villages' – Park Village East and West. Nash, for all his thinking on the grand scale, took care to plan also for the artisans and shopkeepers so essential to a neighbourhood.

The Haymarket itself remained as it was; a busy market for hay and straw, a road in which most of the buildings – apart from the Royal Opera House – were inns and 'ordinaries' serving farmers, waggon drivers and grooms of the many livery stables in the neighbourhood. As well as the Lemon Tree tavern on the corner of Piccadilly, further down there was the Black Horse, the Cock, the George and the Bell. There were also extensive stables behind the Opera House. Parallel with the Haymarket, the part of the new street now called Lower Regent Street was lined with imposing buildings, one of which, No. 14, was John Nash's own residence. It had a magnificent long gallery where he gave

Regent Street Quadrant with the colonnades, 1827 (above); and Verrey's, established the previous year on its present site in Regent Street, photographed (left) early in the twentieth century.

lavish parties graced and glamorized by the Carlton House set. From Piccadilly Circus (at first named Regent Circus South) to Regent Circus North (now Oxford Circus) the new street was to be a shopping street, the first in London to be so planned from the drawing-board, as distinct from *becoming* a shopping street. It was Nash's intention that it should rival and surpass Bond Street, 'that the stream of fashion be diverted to a new Street, where the Footpath will be 15 feet wide, instead of 7 feet, and the Carriage-way double the width of that in Bond-street, and where there will be room for all the fashionable shops to be assembled in one Street.' The shops were to be on the ground floor of the buildings, the shopkeepers and their families living on the mezzanine floor, the floors above to be let as expensive lodgings for visitors to London or as apartments for bachelors and beaux, such as Charles Dickens' Lord Frederick Verisopht and his friend Sir Mulberry Hawk who lodged in 'a handsome suite of private apartments in Regent Street'. Apartments near the Quadrant were much favoured by visiting operatic celebrities.

No butchers, greengrocers, or other domestic trades were to be allowed; no hawkers nor street vendors; no public houses. According to the *Reminiscences of an Old Draper*, 'the majority of people who first opened shops there could not make them answer, let them try never so hard'. Early bankruptcies probably caused some relaxation of the rules, since Thomas Reid, bread and biscuit baker, opened a shop on the west side of Regent Street in 1823 – surely a domestic trade? But this was a marginal case, perhaps, since Reid may also have sold cakes and confectionery, and, according to Whittock's *The Complete Book of Trades*, such shops were often 'fashionable lounging places for the great and titled ones, and the places of assignation for supposed casual encounters – and they were therefore fairly luxurious'.

Although no public houses were permitted, there was no rule against restaurants. Verrey's was established in 1826 on the site it still occupies. Although it was always a respectable establishment (no assignations or casual encounters), Jane Welsh Carlyle nevertheless felt herself rather daring to dine there alone. She wrote to her husband:

I got into a Holborn omnibus after, which left me at the top of Regent Street; and then I went to Verey's [sic] and had – a beautiful little mutton chop and glass of bitter ale! *That* is the sort of thing I do! It was my second dinner at Verey's. . . . The '*chaarge*' is very moderate, and the cooking *perfect*. For my dinner and ale today I paid one-and-fivepence. . . . It amuses me, all that, besides keeping me in health; and for the outrage to '*delicate femaleism*', I am beyond all such considerations at present. However, I see single women besides myself at Verey's – not improper – governesses, and the like.

Two elegant shopping arcades were built while Regent Street was being completed. The Royal Opera Arcade, opened in 1817, was designed by John Nash and George Repton as part of the King's Opera House construction in the Haymarket. Running between Pall Mall and Charles II Street, it became a fashionable ambulatory with elite little shops. The Burlington Arcade was built in 1819 on land adjoining the garden of Burlington House. It was designed by Samuel Ware, the

architect who had been redesigning the house for Lord George Cavendish, and he described it as 'a Piazza for all Hardware, Wearing Apparel and Articles not offensive in appearance nor smell'. Above each tiny bijou shop there were living quarters for the shopkeeper. D. H. Lord, men's outfitters at Nos. 66–70, was one of the original tenants and the shop still trades under that name. There were several bonnet shops, one of which, according to the *Survey of London*, used its upper chambers for prostitution, and 'men of position who wished to avoid publicity in their amours dreaded being seen in the vicinity of the Arcade at certain hours'. It was said that girls from Kate Hamilton's night-house near the Haymarket used to haunt the Arcade during the daytime, 'ready at a given signal to dart into a nearby shop whose upper floors had rooms furnished to their taste and for their purpose'. Queen Street, off Regent Street, was well known for the many French girls who had lodgings there. Jeff's Bookshop in the Burlington Arcade sold nothing but French novels and was visited mainly by men, but also by 'independent women'. It was there, in 1851, that Mary Ann Evans (George Eliot) first met George Henry Lewes, with whom in 1854 she formed a lasting union without marriage until his death twenty-four years later.

In spite of the upper rooms and the French novels, there were strict rules governing the Arcade, enforced by beadles on duty until closing time at 8 o'clock. The closing time is now 5.30, but the rules have never been repealed. It is forbidden to whistle, sing or play a musical instrument in the arcade, to carry a bulky package or an open umbrella. One must not run, nor push a perambulator. A bell is rung at closing time and the gates are locked. The arcade passed to Lord George Cavendish's grandson, Lord Chesham, and remained in the Chesham family until 1926. Since the First World War the beadles have been recruited from the 10th Royal Hussars, Lord Chesham's regiment, a tradition continued by subsequent owners to this day.

In 1859, Augustus Sala described the Arcade as 'a sublimate of superfluities, a booth transplanted bodily from Vanity Fair', and went on:

I don't think there is a shop in its *enceinte* where they sell anything that we could not do without. Boots and shoes are sold there, to be sure, but what boots and shoes? Varnished and embroidered and be-ribboned figments, fitter for a fancy ball or a lady's chamber, there to caper to the jingling melody of a lute, than for serious pedestrianism. Paintings and lithographs for gilded boudoirs, collars for puppy dogs, and silver-mounted whips for spaniels; pocket handkerchiefs, in which an islet of cambric is surrounded by an ocean of lace, embroidered garters and braces, filigree flounces, firework-looking bonnets; scent bottles, sword-knots, brocaded sashes, worked dressing-gowns, inlaid snuff boxes and falbalas of all descriptions; these form the stock-in-trade of the merchants who have here their tiny *boutiques*.

Sala's miscellany of superfluities missed out the miniature delights of Morel's famous toy shop at No. 50, established there a year after the arcade was opened. Morel, besides selling clockwork trains, teddy bears and other favourites, specialized in ivory and silver miniatures, doll's house furniture and minuscule animals in wood, china and glass. The shop was a collector's El Dorado until its closure in 1951. Queen Mary used to call at Morel's to choose furnishings for her famous doll's house, now at the Victoria & Albert Museum; and the Duke of Windsor, when Prince of Wales, used to buy toys there for his little nieces, Princess Margaret Rose and the future Queen Elizabeth II.

Bond Street did not suffer as its shopkeepers had feared from the competition of Regent Street. The publicity London's magnificent new street received on the Continent as well as in England attracted wealthy cosmopolitan shoppers, and the whole area prospered exceedingly,

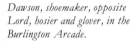
Dawson, shoemaker, opposite Lord, hosier and glover, in the Burlington Arcade.

including the streets linking Regent Street with Bond Street. It was Soho that suffered. There were very few entering streets to it from Regent Street – indeed, this was part of the plan. It was intended that Regent Street should make a firm eastern boundary to aristocratic Mayfair. Beyond this boundary Soho, previously so favoured as a residential quarter and for its speciality shops, began to deteriorate into a quarter for unsuccessful artists, actors and immigrants, a place for seedy night-houses, shady solicitors' offices and rooms to be rented by the hour. Golden Square is described in *Nicholas Nickleby* as

Burlington Arcade: from its opening in 1819 a fashionable place to walk and shop; early in the next century it was a music-hall symbol of smartness through the song 'Burlington Bertie'.

one of the squares that have been; a quarter of the town that has gone down in the world, and taken to letting lodgings. Many of its first and second floors are let, furnished, to single gentlemen; and it takes boarders besides. It is a great resort of foreigners. . . . Two or three violins and a wind instrument from the Opera band reside within its precincts. On a summer's night, windows are thrown open, and groups of swarthy mustachioed men are seen by the passer-by, lounging at the casements and smoking fearfully. Sounds of gruff voices practising vocal music invade the evening's silence.

One could say that Regent Street made an effective *cordon sanitaire* to this Bohemian quarter that had once been so fashionable. The days when it became modish to dine at intimate little Soho restaurants were far ahead.

Exeter Change, looking west towards Charing Cross. Its many attractions included The Royal Menagerie – 'The wild beasts are fed at 6 every evening'. Demolished in 1830.

The Strand had also lost caste, its shopkeepers dealing in fashion goods or exclusive specialities having moved westwards to be in the Regent Street ambience. The Strand's greatest attractions now were Exeter Change and the Lowther Arcade. The Lowther Arcade, during the first half of the nineteenth century, was the great place for toys, a children's paradise, recalled with affection in the memoirs of many Victorian writers. Mrs Carlyle, however, wrote it off as a 'rubbishy place' in a letter to Helen Welsh from Lord Ashburton's house, where she was spending Christmas. Describing the distribution of presents from the Christmas tree in the servants' hall to the forty-eight children of the village school, she wrote:

The whole 48 presents had cost just £2.12.6, having been bought in the Lowther Arcade, the most rubbishy place in London, with a regard to expense that would have been meritorious in the like of us, but which seemed to me – what shall I say? – incomprehensible – in a person with an income of £40,000 a year, and who gives balls at the cost of £700 each.

The Lowther Arcade, 1883: children's paradise.

The character of Holborn had also changed. Although it retained its reputation as a shopping street well into the first quarter of the nineteenth century, it had long lost out as a good private address. Fanny Burney's *Evelina* was published in 1778, and in it Evelina suffers agonies of shame at having to tell Lord Orville she is lodging in Holborn:

'Will Miss Anville allow me to ask her address, and to pay my respects to her before I leave town?' What was the mortification I suffered in answering, 'My Lord, I am – in Holborn!'

On another occasion it is Sir Clement Willoughby to whom is revealed her mortifying address, when he shares a coach with Evelina's vulgar shopkeeping cousins, the Branghtons: 'When, at last, we stopped at an *hosier's* in *High Holborn*, Sir Clement said nothing, but his *eyes*, I saw, were very busily employed in viewing the place, and the situation of the house.'

There is a factual account of the later decline of Holborn as a shopping street in *Reminiscences of an Old Draper*. Looking back to the shop he acquired in Holborn in the early 1830s, William Ablett wrote,

It was not such an attractive market for drapery goods as it had been. There seemed not to be, indeed, that great body of customers having family wants that needed supplying by the local draper; no steady connexion that consumed the whole range of drapery goods that were got through in other places. . . . Tottenham-court-road, where Mr James Shoolbred was doing a large trade and others as well, Oxford Street, and different districts, were all tapping the source from which the old Holborn stream of customers had been derived.

James Shoolbred came to Tottenham Court Road in 1817. His drapery business had been established three years earlier as Shoolbred, Cook & Co., the Cook of the partnership being a brother of the founder of Cook & Sons, wholesale outfitters, of St Paul's Churchyard. The move to Tottenham Court Road was a shrewd one. The builder Thomas Cubitt, who had already been developing much of Camden Town, Stoke Newington and Highbury, had negotiated contracts with the Duke of Bedford for development in north Bloomsbury; Bedford Square, Russell Square, Tavistock Square and Gordon Square, with connecting roads, had all been completed by 1814. Gower Street, running parallel with Tottenham Court Road, had a number of good shops, and Woburn Walk was designed in 1822 purely as a shopping street to serve the prosperous professional families moving into north Bloomsbury. Shoolbred's premises swiftly expanded from a small shop into a building comprising three houses, Nos 154–6 Tottenham Court Road, fronted with two-storied windows supported by graceful Ionic columns. Carpets and soft furnishings were added to the original drapery and outfitting goods and, a little later, groceries and toys. By the mid-nineteenth century, it was a department store boarding five hundred employees, with a reputation for very high-class goods.

The success of Shoolbred's attracted other retailers to Tottenham Court Road, notably Maple's, exactly next door to Shoolbred, in 1841. Two years earlier, a property known as Miller's Stables, a little further south at No. 196, had been taken by John Harris Heal, whose father, also John Harris Heal, came to London from Gillingham, Dorset, in 1805. The latter had first worked with a feather-dressing firm in Leicester Square, then in 1810 had set up a mattress-making business of his own at 33 Rathbone Place. On his death in 1833, his widow Fanny carried on the business until in 1840 her son took over control and organized the move to Miller's Stables. The family lived in an old farm house behind the shop, which later was used as a salesmen's hostel, and remained until 1913. Throughout the 1840s, Heal advertisements appeared in the weekly parts, as they were published, of the novels of Charles Dickens; and by the mid-fifties the business was extended to include bedroom furniture and upholstery as well as mattresses. Adjacent properties were gradually acquired, and in 1854 the entire premises were rebuilt.

With the growing prestige of Shoolbred's, Maple's and Heal's, Tottenham Court Road became known for furniture, and attracted more firms to open shops there. Many individual master cabinet-makers, some depending chiefly for orders from retailers, had their workshops in the network of little streets bounded by Tottenham Court Road, Goodge Street, Berners Street and Oxford Street. At the Tottenham Court Road end of Oxford Street itself, there was after 1761 the London branch of the famous Gillow of Lancaster; and at Nos. 37 and 38, Jackson & Graham, upholsterers and cabinet-makers, also sold carpets, bronzes and porcelains. Arthur Sanderson & Sons, founded in 1860 in Soho Square as suppliers under Royal Warrant of wall coverings, fabric and paints and importers of French wall-hangings, moved to 52 Berners Street in 1864. This concentration of furnishing interests in one area was an example of the manner in which a particular quarter, through the establishment there of one or two firms of particular merit in a particular line of business, attracted other firms of the same or ancillary trades.

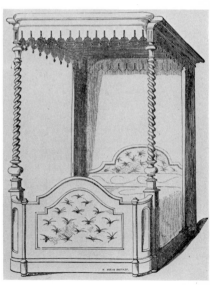

Heal's of Tottenham Court Road, photographed in May 1855. Three years earlier their catalogue was offering a 'Four-Post Bedstead of Elaborate and Chaste Design' for £35.

10 Belgravia – horse omnibuses – shops in novels

*A discreet advertisement for
the royal shawl manufacturers,
J. & J. Holmes.*

SOON AFTER the completion of Regent Street, the boundary of the West End was pushed further westward by an aristocratic extension on land belonging to Lord Grosvenor. When George III, on his accession, bought Buckingham House and had it rebuilt as a royal palace, the land to the west of the royal garden was rough water-logged pasturage known as the Five Fields of Chelsea. Thomas Cubitt, developer of the Duke of Bedford's north Bloomsbury land, realized that the near presence of royalty bestowed a potential residential value upon those soggy fields. So he leased the land from Lord Grosvenor, devised a way of draining it, then raised its level with earth being dug out to make St Katharine's dock by the Tower of London. The earth was brought upstream in barges to Millbank, where Cubitt had a depot. This preliminary work done, in 1827 he laid out one of the largest, most lordly squares in London, Belgrave Square, and the following year began upon the even more grandiose Eaton Square. Thus was Belgravia born.

Elegant connecting streets and crescents linked the squares with Ebury Street to the south, Grosvenor Place to the east, to the north with Knightsbridge, and to the west with Hans Town. This was a 'little town' or residential estate previously almost isolated in open country. The land had been leased in 1770 from Lord Cadogan by the architect Henry Holland, and he named the little town in honour of his father-in-law Sir Hans Sloane, as also Hans Place, Sloane Street and Sloane Square. Of Cadogan Place, Dickens wrote in *Nicholas Nickleby*:

It is the one slight bond that joins two great extremes; it is the connecting link between the aristocratic pavements of Belgrave Square and the barbarism of Chelsea. . . . The people in Cadogan Place look down upon Sloane Street, and think Brompton low. . . . Not that they claim to be on precisely the same footing as the high folks of Belgrave Square and Grosvenor Place, but that they stand with reference to them rather in the light of those illegitimate children of the great who are content to boast of their connexions, although their connexions disavow them.

Thackeray chose Grosvenor Place for the socially ambitious Amorys when they rented a house for the Season, hoping to buy their way into Society with lavish entertaining.

Through-traffic was banned from the Belgrave estate. There were bars across the entering roads, attended by top-hatted beadles who turned away commercial vehicles and unauthorized private carriages. Public houses were only allowed in the mews, and naturally no retail trade was permitted to taint Belgravia. It is true that in 1830 Seth Smith built a two-storied bazaar named the Pantechnicon in Motcombe Street, Belgravia; but its retail activities were disguised by it being described as an exhibition place for 'all kinds of artistic work'. It later became a saleroom for carriages and furniture, all clearly ticketed with prices; and there was a wine department and a toy department. When in 1844, Charles Dickens was preparing to transfer his whole family to a rented villa at Albaro, Italy, he went to the Pantechnicon to buy a commodious travelling carriage. He chose a heavy vehicle, requiring four horses to draw it. It was priced at £60, but he got it for £45 cash down. In Marylebone there was the Baker Street Bazaar, which began as a 'horse bazaar', but after horses ceased 'to be exposed here for sale', the chief commodities became carriages and harness. It seems to have captured most of the carriage trade, since by the 1860s the Pantechnicon in Belgravia was concentrating upon furniture. Indeed, it was so connected with furniture in the public mind, that the Pantechnicon vans gradually had their name given to any furniture van. Furniture depositories also

Setting out from Belgravia.

adopted the name – in the 1880s, for example, the Kensington Pantechnicon at 8 King Street, near the High Street.

For household marketing undertaken by the staff of Belgravian households there were provision shops in the little streets to the south – and, of course, Fortnum & Mason delivered. The ladies of Belgravia drove in their broughams or barouches to Regent Street and Bond Street for personal shopping. Indeed, to drive to Regent Street in the afternoon was a compulsion – not so much to shop as to be seen, for it had become a fashionable parade ground. John Tallis's London street guide of 1838 described the scene: 'For Regent Street to be seen to the best advantage, it should be visited on a summer's day in the afternoon, when the splendid carriages, and elegantly attired pedestrians, evince the opulence and taste of our magnificent metropolis.' No tiresome people at that time would question whether opulence and taste could go together.

Although the first retailers to take shops in Regent Street had found business disappointing, even disastrous, once the whole street had been completed it became the most splendid display-case for luxury merchandise, a shopping street beyond the dreams of avarice. When General Blucher was visiting London he is said to have exclaimed, on being driven down Regent Street: 'What a place to loot!' Augustus Sala wrote of the shops being 'innately fashionable . . . indeed, Regent Street is an avenue of superfluities, a great trunk-road in Vanity Fair. Fancy watchmakers, haberdashers, and photographers; fancy stationers, fancy hosiers, and fancy staymakers; music shops, shawl shops, jewellers, French glove shops, perfumery, and point-lace shops, confectioners and milliners; creamily, these are the merchants whose wares are exhibited in this bezesteen of the world.'

One of the earliest fashion shops in the street was the shawl warehouse of J. & J. Holmes. In Mrs Bell's *World of Fashion* it was described as 'the most splendid establishment even in that vicinage, deserving the flattering encomiums bestowed on it by the fashionables who visit it.' They sold shawls from one guinea to a hundred guineas and held the Royal Appointment to HM the Queen, HRH The Duchess of Kent, and several other HRHs. It was a great period for shawls –

Holmes had at least four rivals in Regent Street alone. One of them was T. Williams' India and British Cloak and Shawl Warehouse at Regent Circus, with other premises at Nos. 211–13, specialists in Oriental and Sultan long shawls. This house, like Waithman's of Ludgate Hill, not only sold shawls, but bought and exchanged them, and had a customers' cleaning service. In Fleet Street, Howes & Hart's India Warehouse tried to attract customers away from the West End by advertising in the *Morning Herald* of 30 October 1835: 'Ladies with carriages are respectfully informed that the above establishment is situated only sixty doors from Temple-bar, and the approach from the West is remarkably good, since the great improvement made in the thoroughfare by the widening of the Strand.'

This widening had only just been completed in 1835, not before it was needed. Traffic in all main streets had become a major problem since the introduction of horse omnibuses. There were no prescribed stopping places for them, passengers being put down and taken up wherever they wished, while other vehicles snarled up behind them. It had been in 1829 that the first horse omnibus, pioneered by a coachmaker named George Shillibeer, travelled from the Yorkshire Stingo in Lisson Grove to the Bank of England, going along the New Road and Holborn. It brought cheap and frequent transport to a long corridor of middle-class housing, and Shillibeer thoughtfully provided free middle-class newspapers for his passengers to read while in traffic jams. This was the beginning of London's public transport. Between 1830 and 1837 four hundred horse omnibuses went into use on various routes. They brought the residents of London's surrounding villages into touch with the West End shops. Sophie and Fanny Horsley, who lived with their parents near the gravel pits on Campden Hill above Kensington High Street, in the 1830s made quite frequent trips to London in George Chancellor's omnibus,

Farmer & Rogers succeeded J. & J. Holmes at 171–9 Regent Street. Their 'Great Shawl & Cloak Emporium' added travelling dresses, opera jackets and croquet jackets to the immense range of shawls. Arthur Liberty worked here from 1862 until he opened his own shop in 1875.

which set them down in Piccadilly at the corner of Bond Street. They also shopped locally at Breeze & James, a drapery shop established in Kensington High Street in 1810 and patronized by the Duchess of Kent and the Princess Victoria when they lived at Kensington Palace. After Victoria's marriage, Breeze & James named their business Coburg House as a compliment to Prince Albert of Saxe-Coburg. There was also, early in the century, Mr Smith's bonnet shop in the High Street; but the Horsley sisters did not consider his creations sufficiently distinguished for special occasions and would take the omnibus to Alabaster's 'Straw and Fancy Hat Shop' in Piccadilly to find something really *à la mode*.

Hansom cabs were introduced in 1834 and were an immediate success with people who had used the slow, jolting 'glass coaches' previously on hire. But the gentry also made use of omnibuses. On 16 January 1835 Creevey wrote to Miss Ord: 'What dear things omnibuses are! I was at Greenwich at 2 o'clock; then came in one to Charing Cross . . . then got into an omnibus at the top of St. James's Street in Piccadilly, and went to Lad Lane in the City . . . then got on another omnibus and was landed in the same place in Piccadilly . . . whole cost of the day two shillings.' Mrs Carlyle was another omnibus enthusiast: 'I went in an omnibus to Putney yesterday evening, and came back outside. It is as pleasant as a barouche and four, the top of an omnibus, but the conductors don't like the trouble of helping one up.' In a letter to Jeannie Welsh in January 1843 she tells of going by omnibus to buy tea and coffee at Fortnum & Mason, and when it came on to rain of 'making for the nearest refuge, the London Library'. It seems to eliminate the century and a half between Jane Carlyle and ourselves that we can still do exactly that: take a bus from Chelsea to Piccadilly, get off at Fortnum & Mason, walk down to the London Library in St James's Square.

The fame of London's omnibuses spread abroad. But when Francis Wey visited England in the 1850s he was disappointed:

We had heard so much about the London omnibuses, with their velvet upholstery and veneered panelling, that we were anxious to see these wonderful conveyances. So our amazement was great on boarding one in the Strand to find it narrow, rickety, jolting, dusty and extremely dirty. The only advantage of these vehicles is that they are closed by a door. The conductor stands outside on a small footboard, incessantly hailing the passers-by. The custom, anyhow, is never to go inside an omnibus, even when it rains, if there is an inch of space unoccupied outside; women, children, even old people, fight to gain access to the top.

No doubt the Strand and City omnibuses were more crowded than those serving rural Chelsea and Putney that Mrs Carlyle used. From 1846 when a two-penny fare was introduced, far more people could afford to use them regularly – before omnibuses had been too expensive for working people. They walked to work, and anything up to five miles was quite normal.

The lack of any cheap transport was one of the factors that caused big shops to have living-in quarters for their staff. The smaller dressmaking and millinery establishments expected their women workers and girl

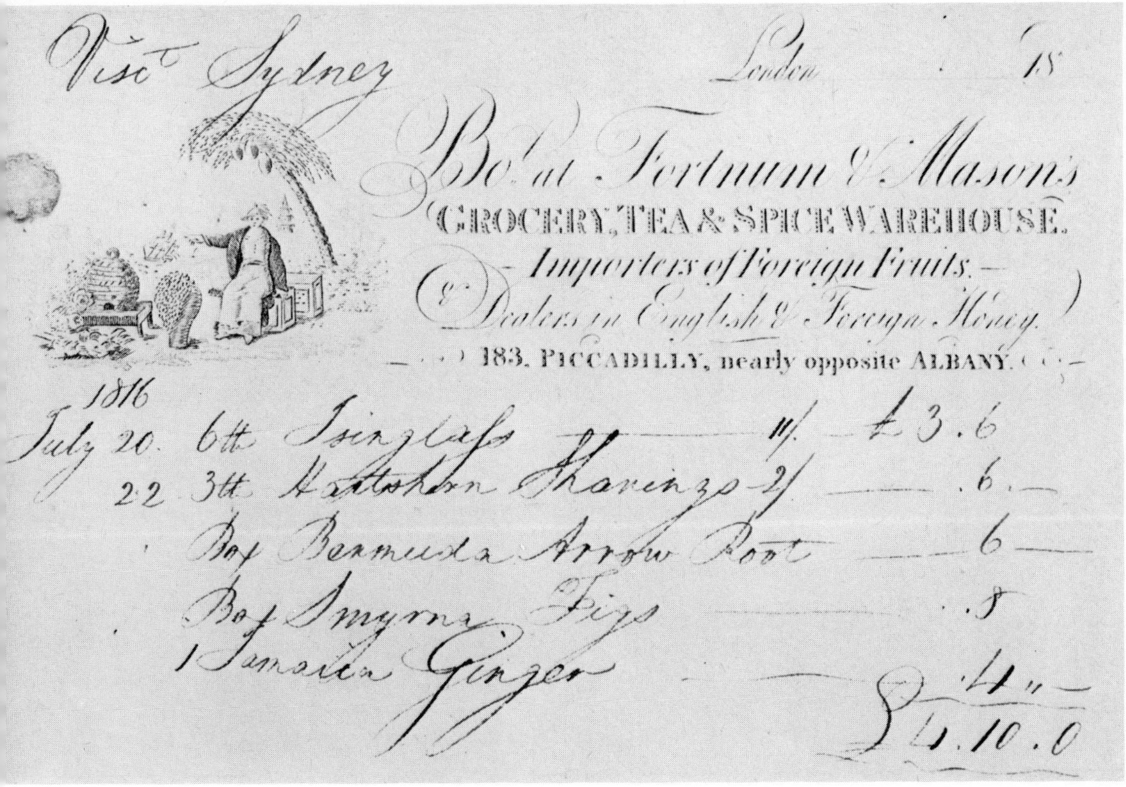
Visct Sydney London 18

Bot at Fortnum & Mason's
GROCERY, TEA & SPICE WAREHOUSE.
Importers of Foreign Fruits.
& Dealers in English & Foreign Honey.
183, PICCADILLY, nearly opposite ALBANY.

1816 July 20.	6lb Isinglass	11/	£3.6
22	3lb Hartshorn Shavings	2/	.6.
	Box Bermuda Arrow Root		6
	Box Smyrna Figs		.8
	1 Jamaica Ginger		4
			£4.10.0

Viscount Sydney's bill at Fortnum & Mason, 1816. Among the purchases: Jamaica ginger, Smyrna figs and Bermuda arrow-root.

apprentices to live at home with their families. When Kate Nickleby worked at Madame Mantalini's in Cavendish Square, she walked every morning all the way from her mother's lodgings in Thames Street, by one of the City wharfs, and her mother came on foot in the dark evenings to escort her home. It is rather surprising that Dickens should have sited Madame Mantalini's dressmaking establishment in a residential square. Certainly there was no shop window. The showrooms were on the first floor and workrooms above, with Madame and her Italian gigolo living on the ground floor. Nevertheless, there was a brass plate at the door, so it seems that trade was permitted in elite Cavendish Square – unless, of course, Dickens made a mistake.

Dickens did not introduce the names of real shops in his novels, as did Thackeray and some of the earlier writers of fashionable novels, notably Mrs Gore. Mrs Gore brought in so many names that the *Westminster Review* (October 1831), in a long critical notice of *Pin Money*, accused her of 'puffing' shops to her personal advantage:

A book like *Pin Money* is, in fact, a sort of London Directory. . . . We are not sure the authoress of this work has made any bargain with her tradespeople; but we are very certain she might. None of the persons commemorated would hesitate to give a popular authoress the run of the shop, for the sake of being down in her list; we are too much out of the world to know whether what we are suggesting may not be quite common practice; and we may be recommending what is done every day, and what would really seem to be done on every page. If not, what can be meant by such advertisements as these?

'Twice she rose and seized the embossed blotting-book (that prettiest of Harding's importations).'

This is a puff assuredly worth an embossed blotting-book; and of course Mr. Harding has sent one to the authoress; if not, we, who see the advantage of this new kind of advertisement *orné*, would advise Mrs. Gore to strike the ungrateful wretch from her list.

'Good morning Mr. Storr! – what put it into your head to send in my bill? I have not the least idea of paying it.'

'Whenever you please Madam!'

Does not this, in the plainest manner, announce that Messrs. Storr and Mortimer are accommodating creditors; and give any length of credit that may be agreeable to ladies of fashion?

'I expect a man with silks from Harding's (*query the same Harding – Mrs. Gore should add an appendix of addresses*). At half-past one, Mawe's people are coming to clean my alabaster vases; at two, Ridgeway's clerk will come here to see how many of the pamphlets I keep.'

Silks, alabaster vases, and pamphlets; now here are three necessaries of life pointed out; and not merely as to the fact where they may be had. But further – Harding will send silks to be seen; Mawe will clean vases, and Ridgeway will let you have his publications on sale or return!

Ridgeway's bookshop in Piccadilly was patronized by Lord Byron, who paid a bill of over £133 there in 1813. How long it had been mounting up we do not know.

This 'puffing' of tradesmen (whether or not for goods and services received), although deplored by critical reviewers, may have been very helpful to the newly rich from the industrial north in telling them which London shops were patronized by Society. Mrs Gore's contemporary Thackeray parodied in *Punch* what he saw as an obsession with titled characters in her novels, but he did not attack her for 'puffing'. He was not, after all, guiltless himself. He mentions Fortnum & Mason twice in *Pendennis*, and also Gillow the furnishing firm – 'mansions to be had unfurnished, where, if you have credit with Messrs. Gillow or Bantings, you can get them splendidly *montées* and decorated entirely according to your own fancy.' Gillow was decidedly the most highly esteemed furnishing firm. Mrs Gore brings the name into *Mothers and Daughters*, published in 1831. A waggish wit is talking of the extravagance of young Lord Stapylford: 'Do you know, Miss Lorimer, that Gillow has fitted up Stapylford's kennel with mahogany stalls and hair mattresses?' Thackeray writes in *Vanity Fair* of Joe Sedley's man-servant 'marking his victim down, as you see one of Mr. Paynter's assistants in Leadenhall Street ornament an unconscious turtle with a placard on which is written SOUP TOMORROW'. Again, he writes of Sir Pitt Crawley's sideboard being covered with 'old cups, both gold and silver; old salvers and cruet-stands, like Rundell & Bridge's shop'.

Rundell & Bridge, established on Ludgate Hill in 1788, was one of the most fashionable goldsmiths and jewellers. We learn from Doris Langley Moore's *Lord Byron – Accounts Rendered* that they paid £1,130 cash for Mrs Byron's jewels after her death in 1811. Captain Gronow wrote of Rundell & Bridge being patronized by the great for extravagant jewellery to give to their mistresses and 'obtaining large sums of money from their enamoured clients for whom they often became bankers'. Rundell & Bridge closed down in 1843, and that April Mrs Gore wrote a sixty-line poem of protest in *Ainsworth's Magazine*. This is the beginning:

On Seeing an Advertisement of the Intended Retirement of an Eminent Firm

> *Retire from business? – shut up shop? –*
> *Rundell and Bridge! – I charge ye, stop!*
>   *Think twice ere ye determine!*
> *If you suspend your handiworks,*
> *Where shall we find our spoons and forks –*
>   *Where diamonds to our ermine?*
> *Reflect on all the happy pairs*
> *Your plain gold rings have wrung with cares*
>   *In matrimonial trammel;*
> *Reflect how many a cruel hoax*
> *You've played on legacy-hunting folks*
>   *In black and gold enamel!*
> *Think with what vile considerations*
> *You've influenced the fate of nations,*
>   *By diamond snuff-box treason!*
> *How you have raised the price, per carat.*
> *Of royal phizzes, which men stare at,*
>   *Or, if the snuff wills, sneeze on!*
> *Admit how many a joyous girl,*
> *Bribed by your strings of Orient pearl –*
>   *The trappings of a bride –*
> *To glitter like Golconda's queen,*
> *Hath to a loathing duchess been*
>   *Sadly transmogrified!*

Another shop mentioned in Mrs Gore's novels was that of Howell & James, the breakaway partnership from Harding, Howell & Co. of Schomberg House. Their shop in Lower Regent Street flourished. Besides silks and other fabrics, they sold glass, china, furnishings, jewellery and – rather unexpectedly – wine. It was Howell & James who in 1849 precipitated the collapse of Lady Blessington's glittering but equivocal ménage at Gore House. This they did by putting in an execution for a debt of some thousands of pounds that Lady Blessington had incurred when furnishing Gore House thirteen years earlier, thereby firing the starting gun for all her other creditors to foreclose. That the firm had waited for thirteen years is indicative of the long credit granted by shops to distinguished customers – the long credit being reflected, of course, in high prices. It is surprising that Mrs Carlyle, who was not of the aristocracy nor in Society, a lady decidedly careful with money and accustomed to paying cash, should have gone to Howell & James for a gown. In a letter to her husband in 1858 she wrote of the Howell & James dressmaker having 'padded the new gown in a very artistic manner'. But she was writing when she was a guest at Lady Ashburton's

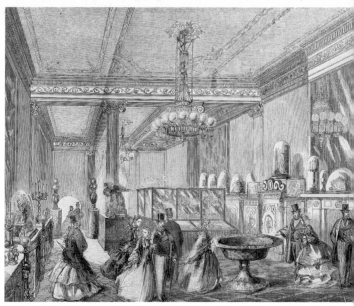

The exterior of Howell & James in Regent Street, 1849, and their impressive showroom, which exhibited ceramics, silverware, jewellery and antiques; other rooms showed furnishings and dress silks.

Bay House, and the extravagance may have been decided upon as a boost to her self-confidence on the visit. Howell & James supplied silks to Queen Victoria, 24 yards to each dress length – 'very ample proportions', as the department buyer who took them to Buckingham Palace noted.

It was the custom at Howell & James for coachmen and footmen, while waiting for their ladies, to go down the steps to the area under the shop window, where they were served with free beer and bread and cheese. We do not know whether the custom held good during the annual exhibitions of ceramic work by amateurs held at the shop and patronized by Queen Victoria and other members of the royal family. According to one of their advertisements, 'The Exhibition of 1878 contained upwards of one thousand original works, mostly by ladies, and was frequented during its two months duration by nearly 10,000 visitors.' The firm undertook the firing of amateurs' pieces, and Geoffrey Godden in his *Victorian Porcelain* says that examples of amateurs' work can occasionally be found still bearing the original paper label of Howell & James, giving details of the painter, source of design and date.

The shop that was mentioned in novels more often than any other throughout the nineteenth century was Gunter's. The business was founded in 1757 by an Italian pastrycook, Domenico Negri, who later took Gunter into partnership 'making and selling all sorts of English, French and Italian wet and dry sweetmeats, Cedrati and Bergamet Chips, and Naples Divolini, at the sign of the Pot and Pineapple in Berkeley Square'. A pineapple was the emblem generally adopted by eighteenth-century confectioners. Gunter's was celebrated also for its turtle soup, made from turtles killed in Honduras. The original shop was at No. 7 on the east side of Berkeley Square, four doors away from Horace

Walpole's house. Much later it was moved to the corner of Curzon Street and Park Lane. At all Society balls and receptions catering was by Gunter; and the firm's activities were not confined to London. Mrs Gore wrote of Gunter 'taxing his exhausted imagination for the caramel novelties of a fête champêtre'; and Creevey wrote on 1 July 1829 of the appalling weather at the Horticultural Fête: 'Poor Gunter says the Ladies drank so freely to keep the cold out, that he shall be a decided loser by his contract.'

Gunter's ices were famous, made by a secret recipe. But deliveries of ice depended upon winds and tides. On 5 July 1827 *The Times* carried an announcement: 'Messrs Gunter respectfully beg to inform the nobility and gentry who honour them with their custom that this day having received one of their cargoes of ice by the *Platoff* from the Greenland seas, they are enabled to supply their cream fruit ices at their former prices'. In hot summer weather, it was the custom for ladies to recline in their elegant equipages under the trees on the *opposite* side of Berkeley Square from Gunter's shop, while waiters scurried to and fro with trays of ices. Gunter's was the only place of refreshment in London where it was perfectly correct for a lady to be seen alone with a gentleman during the afternoon. On 18 August 1843, Jane Carlyle wrote to her husband: 'Darwin came yesterday after my dinner time (I had dined at three), and remarked, in the course of some speculative discourse, that I "looked as if I needed to go to Gunter's and have an ice!" Do you comprehend what sort of a look that can be? Certainly he was right, for driving to Gunter's and having an ice revived me considerably.' As it was August, they probably ate their ices outside in the Square. But the elegant equipages would not have been there. The Season was over and Society would have departed to Cowes, to the moors, to the German spas.

Berkeley Square at 5 pm, 24 August 1867.

'*It is under the trees, it is out of the sun,*
In the corner where GUNTER *retails a plum bun.*
Her footman goes once, and her footman goes twice,
Ay, and each time returning he brings her an ice.'

117

Mid-century Regent Street. The destruction of the colonnades in 1848 (top left) was deplorable, but the street continued to be the vortex of fashionable shopping (below left, in 1849). The scene in 1852 (top right) shows Swan & Edgar's corner on Piccadilly Circus; and Peter Robinson, established since 1833 on Oxford Circus (below right, photographed 1910), in the mid-fifties opened a separate Mourning House in Regent Street.

11 Mid-Victorian Regent Street

FOR THE RAILWAY.

Scott Adie of Regent Street supplies the needs of the railway age – 'Open the Maud out full size, take it in the centre and bring it over your head from behind.'

TWO YEARS before Victoria's accession, Dickins & Smith, who had in 1790 opened a drapery shop at 54 Oxford Street under the sign of the Golden Lion, moved to Regent Street, which had become the magnet for all ambitious shopkeepers. Taking their Golden Lion sign with them, they set up in premises opposite the Hanover Chapel, and named them Hanover House. They also took another partner and became Dickins, Smith & Stevens. In a later reorganization, they were to become Dickins & Jones. The Golden Lion sign remained until the rebuilding of Regent Street in the 1920s, and the rebuilt store on the same site is still called Dickins & Jones.

Nearby, on the corner of Regent Street and Little Argyll Street, there was the building that from 1806 to 1830 had been the Argyll Rooms. Promoted, according to the *Survey of London*, 'by a wellborn scallywag', the Rooms seem to have had 'some of the decorative distinction still at this time thought appropriate to the pursuit of pleasure'. But by the 1830s, Society was pursuing its pleasure elsewhere, and the Argyll Rooms – with their decorative distinction – were acquired, first by Charles Cook's Fur Company, and then in 1854 by Nicholson's of St Paul's. Nicholson was the most important retail draper in the City, and it was as the Argyll Mourning Warehouse that he opened his Regent Street acquisition. One might say the Argyll Rooms suffered a swift descent from the promotion of pleasure to preoccupation with death – death with all the trimmings. According to a contemporary guide-book, the mourning warehouse kept 'the spacious and highly ornamental saloons . . . which are at once chastely elegant and entirely appropriate'.

This was not the first Regent Street shop to specialize in the trappings of grief. Just across the street, Jay's General Mourning Warehouse had been opened in 1841 – a magnificent establishment occupying the whole of three houses, Nos. 247–9. Further down the street, at No. 173, Pugh's Mourning Warehouse was established in 1849; and a little later Peter Robinson took over four houses between the Circus and the Argyll Mourning Warehouse for a branch of his business devoted entirely to mourning clothes. It soon became affectionately known as Black Peter Robinson's. The main Peter Robinson shop was at 103 Oxford Street, almost on the corner of Oxford Circus – in fact, where it is now.

NOVELTIES

AT

JAY'S.

CHANTILLY LACE COSTUME,
ON SATIN FOUNDATION WITH JETTED PANEL,
Including Lace and Trimming for Bodice,
5½ Guineas.

ELEGANT TEA GOWN.
BLACK, OR BLACK AND WHITE CHINA SILK,
5½ Guineas.

Jay's magnificent Mourning Warehouse occupied Nos. 247–9 Regent Street and was, according to the anonymous A Visit to Regent Street, 'an inexhaustible theme for the speculative pen-dashers of the diurnal press'. Above: Jay's mourning gowns of 1888.

Robinson was the son of a Yorkshire haberdasher, who had served his apprenticeship in a small draper's shop in Paddington before setting up as a linen-draper on his own in 1833.

The many shops specializing in mourning clothes were assured of rich pickings from death all the year round, not only at times of Court and national mourning. Middle- and upper-class etiquette demanded that upon a death in a family the whole household must go into mourning, including children and servants. Every species of relative was mourned according to the relationship, distant cousins according to the distance, aunts dependent upon whether they were aunts-in-law or blood aunts. A married woman had to mourn her husband's relatives as well as her own, whether or not she had even met them, much less felt any affection for them. Who to mourn, how deeply and for how long, was a perpetual worry to Lady Stanley of Alderley. In 1844 she wrote to her daughter-in-law who was staying in London: 'I suppose the Court mourning still continues or if not I hope you will put it on for Sir Gregory Way; he is my first cousin and there are several of the family in Town who might observe and be hurt if you did not.' The timing of a relative's death could be exasperating: 'We have just heard of the death of Mrs. Gibson [Lord Stanley's sister] – I thought she would die soon when I got a coloured poplin from Ireland the other day.'

Henry Mayhew recalled going to Jay's with his aunt when he was a small boy:

Below: Nicholson's of St Paul's Churchyard, famous City drapers established 1843, opened a Regent Street branch for mourning clothes in the mid-fifties. Their main shop (shown here after rebuilding in 1900) survived the blitz, but was demolished for the City Barbican in 1963.

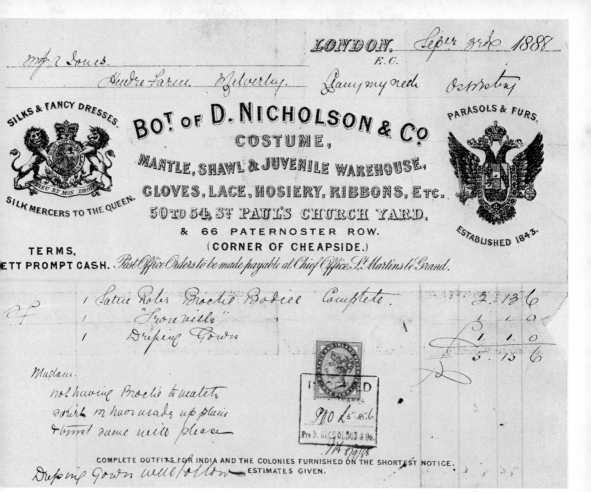

A Nicholson's bill of 1888.

We recollect passing down a long vestibule and up a long flight of steps, and at last emerging in a large, lofty room. This room had tall gothic windows; it was softly carpeted, so that you scarcely heard your own footsteps as you trod along. . . . We noted the quietness, the harmonious so to speak hush of the whole place, and were impressed with the total 'unshoppy' character of the establishment.

Augustus Sala had equally indelible childhood memories of a funeral monument shop in Regent Street, on the corner of Air Street:

with the mural tablets, the obelisks, the broken columns, the extinguished torches, and the draped urns in the window, and some with the inscriptions into the bargain, all ready engraved in black and white, puzzling us as to whether the tender husbands, devoted wives, and affectionate sons, to whom they referred, were buried in that grisly shop – it had a pleasant, fascinating terror about it, like an undertaker's, too.

But all was not black crape and tombstones in Regent Street: far from it. For one thing there were the Scotch Warehouses, shouting their tartan. Queen Victoria was not responsible for the epidemic of 'tartanitis' or 'highland fever', as *Punch* called it, that swept England. Certainly it raged more fiercely after her purchase of Balmoral and the

VIGO STREET.   415   117   119. James Locke,   121   123   125   127. James Locke,   129
                                  Scotch Tartan Warehouse.   Scotch Tweed Warehouse.   Importe

'Highland fever' in Regent Street: James Locke's Scotch Tartan Warehouse at No. 119, and his Scotch Tweed Warehouse at No. 127, in 1849.

beginning of her love affair with the Highlands and Highlanders; but the passion for all things Scottish was aroused in the first place by the Waverley novels of Sir Walter Scott, which were published nearly every year between 1814 and 1831, disseminating romantic ideas about Scotland. Mechanical spinning and weaving techniques of the industrial revolution had made large output possible, and Scots businessmen were not slow to take advantage of the demand for tartans and for the black and white check shepherds' cloak tweed that was becoming all the rage for gentlemen's wraps – and also for fashionable trousers after Sir Walter had appeared in a pair made of finely woven shepherds' check. Moreover, 'highland fever' was not confined to England. After Waterloo there was an epidemic of it in Paris. This can most plausibly be explained by the excitement, once the long wars were over, of being able to import foreign goods, and tartans spoke their country of origin more loudly than any other import. Also, there were old sentimental ties between Scotland and France, created by the sojourns in France of history's most romantic characters, Mary Queen of Scots and the Stuart princes.

Two brothers called Gardiner, Glasgow tailors, came south in 1839 and opened a shop in Aldgate selling Scottish tweeds and tartans, calling it The Scotch House. Sixty-one years later, The Scotch House moved to its present site on the peninsula between Brompton Road and Knightsbridge. Before the end of the 1840s, James Locke opened his Scotch Tweed Warehouse at 127 Regent Street, a branch of the Scotch Tartan Warehouse he had previously established at No. 119. By 1866 he had extended into No. 117 as well. But it was the London Scotch Warehouse of Scott Adie at 115 Regent Street that secured the Royal Appointment. His was a handsome building on the corner of Vigo Street. Over the doorway he erected a gas bracket in the form of a giant thistle, which burst into a blaze of lights as dusk fell, a gas-jet on every

The Scott Adie trade card.

spine of the thistle. This famous landmark remained until the rebuilding of Regent Street, when Scott Adie moved to 38 Conduit Street. Bombed out from there during the Second World War, the shop is now at 14a Clifford Street, still treasuring the last few yards of a bale of cloth from which one of Queen Victoria's cloaks was cut. Confirmation of the Scottish vogue in Paris is given by an early Scott Adie price list written in French as well as English, and by catalogues with French introductions, bearing the motto *Toujours mieux faire coûte que coûte.*

By the mid-nineteenth century, the shops in Regent Street and Bond Street boasting Royal Appointments had multiplied. Not only was there the Queen's own large family to supply, but most of her royal relations in Europe came to London to shop from time to time. At Herbert Johnson, the hatter of New Bond Street, there were as many framed warrants on the walls as hat-boxes on the shelves. At Cartier's, when the shop last had a good spring clean, it was decided to store away the warrants granted by members of dynasties since fallen, and keep on the walls only those still extant. J. Medwin & Co. of 86 Regent Street, who had made boots for the Duke of Wellington, could proudly claim to be not only by appointment to HRH the Prince Consort, but also to the Emperor of the French. Medwin's had created 'The Resilient Boot', based on 'a scientific anatomical knowledge necessary to the perfect construction of a well-fitting boot', and had hoped to get it adopted by the army. The firm wrote a series of letters to *The Times*, the Government and the War Office, pointing out 'the importance of scrupulously attending to certain known laws in regard to the clothing of the feet, and the consequences which could assuredly follow any deviation from these prescribed data. These cautions were unheeded until too late – with the frightful consequences which were attendant upon our bravest soldiers in the Crimean War.'

H. J. & D. Nicoll, established at Nos. 114–20 Regent Street in 1846 (also of Cornhill, and St Ann's Square, Manchester), remained there until Montague Burton bought the business after the Second World War. Army clothiers and paletot patentees, they also undertook ladies' riding habits and chamois leather riding trousers. They anticipated advertising copywriters of a century later in the literary turn of their publicity. This little anecdote about their 'Travelling Portmanteau' is an example:

At 8 this morning, we were awoke by our man-servant presenting a telegram: 'Immediate: You're wanted at Yeovil'. A cup of coffee, a rusk hastily swallowed while dressing. Hansom cab at door. Drive to Nicoll's, rush into their travelling department, seize one of their ready-fitted black portmanteaux, strapped and patent-locked, and just the size to go under the seat of a railway-carriage; pay exactly five pounds for it and its contents. Thus no waiting for change, and at the South-Western with just three minutes to secure cosy corner; open portmanteau at starting, find a velvet travelling-cap folded up in a small compact Russia-leather pocket-case. A warm and comfortable rug for the knees, which, likewise, is fashioned to wear as a waterproof cloak, shaped with pockets and collar, wherewith to cross an unsheltered platform to a refreshment-room, or – happy thought – lend to a fair friend. And, besides these, we find two shirts, three collars, three pairs of socks, one pair of drawers, a flannel waistcoat, razor and case, shaving, nail, tooth and clothes brushes, and Bradshaw's Guide!

Undeniably a good five pounds worth, even when five pounds meant five golden sovereigns.

Nash's graceful colonnade was removed from the Quadrant in 1848. The villain of this piece of vandalism was Mr Frederick Crane of Sandland & Crane, whose invention of gentlemen's patent belt drawers had won the firm a 'world-wide reputation'. Mr Crane was known as 'the father of Regent Street', being the oldest merchant in the street, and the 1887 edition of *Modern London* seems to have considered he did a public service: 'It was he who caused the unsightly colonnade to be removed from the street thirty years ago, and he was an active promoter of many other improvements which had made Regent Street the first thoroughfare in the world'. There are Mr Cranes in every era, campaigning for

Medwin's 'The Resilient Boot'.

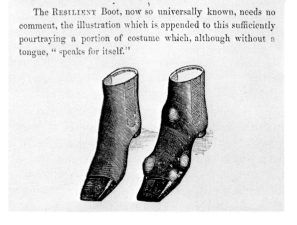

The RESILIENT Boot, now so universally known, needs no comment, the illustration which is appended to this sufficiently pourtraying a portion of costume which, although without a tongue, " speaks for itself."

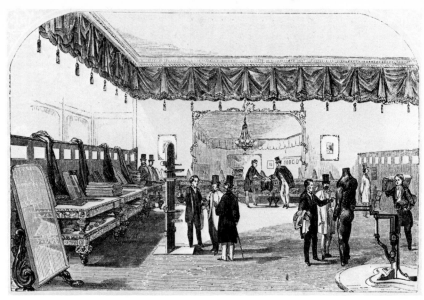

'improvements' that are, quite incidentally of course, of benefit to
traders. But in Augustus Sala's opinion, this Mr Crane not only
desecrated Regent Street, but did himself and his fellow tradespeople no
service: 'Whatever can have possessed our Commissioner of Woods and
Forests to allow those unrivalled arcades to be demolished! The stupid
tradesmen whose purblind, shop-till avarice led them to petition for the
removal of the columns, gained nothing by the change, for the Quadrant
as a lounge in wet weather was at once destroyed; it not only afforded a
convenient shelter beneath, but it was a capital promenade for the
dwellers in the first-floors above.'

Sala was writing in the 1850s, when Regent Street was still a
fashionable parade ground. 'Only here', observed Francis Wey, the
Frenchman who visited London at this time,

could you find the fashionable world so perfectly at home in the middle of the
street. . . . Towards four o'clock, starting from Regents Quadrant and to right
and left of Oxford Street, the crowd surges this way and that; carriages stand in
groups in front of Swan & Edgar's silk shop, or at Allison's, where the latest
fashions and materials are displayed. Buzzing round the carriages are
innumerable horsemen, gentlemen wishing to pay their respects to the ladies.
Regent Street is a precious observatory; it is only there that rank and fashion
can be studied at close quarters in a public place in morning clothes.

Francis Wey was also impressed that in London shops one did not
bargain over prices as in Paris. 'The assistant thinks at first that you have
misunderstood him, but when he realises what you are driving at he
stiffens visibly like a man of honour to whom one has made a shady
proposal. He gives you to understand, politely but plainly, that his prices
being equitable, cannot be reduced.'

The elegant congestion was not only crowded into one time of day,
but into one season of the year. 'With the West End no contrast can well

be greater than that presented by fashion's haunt in and out of the season,' declared the *Illustrated London News* in 1866.

In the former case, all is bustle and gaiety; in the latter, gloom and desolation. The brilliant ever-shifting scene presented daily in Regent Street during the season is dizzying in its confusion ... the fireflies of fashion glance rapidly hither and thither, and the West End streets are thronged with a promiscuous jungle of carriages, horsemen and horsewomen, cabs, omnibuses, and wagons; the pavements being crowded with fashionable loungers. With what dignified ease the gorgeously bedizened footmen attend to their mistresses or lounge about in attitudes of studied grace.

It was estimated in the 1850s that there were 80,000 private carriages in London, and that between the hours of four and six o'clock each day at least 40,000 of them were being driven about the streets and parks. Bond Street, much narrower than Regent Street, suffered the worst traffic jams. Redmayne's, ladies' tailor of 192 New Bond Street and 35 Conduit Street, advertised: 'Ready access will always be found in Conduit Street when Bond Street is blocked.' Also in Conduit Street was the new six-storey building of Lewis & Allenby, silk merchants of 195 Regent Street. This, in the 1860s, was the first building in the West End to be constructed entirely for one retail business; with showrooms, workrooms and living accommodation for the staff. Shop assistants were usually lodged in adjacent or nearby hostels – one-sex hostels, of course.

The living-in system was a natural development from the custom of apprentices living with their masters' families. It must be remembered that many shop assistants were youths from the provinces who had either been apprenticed in their home-towns before seeking a position in the capital, or who had been apprenticed as boys in London. It was essential that they should be lodged and looked after; but as they grew older, the paternal system irked. The hostels had all the rules of Victorian institutions. Indeed, they became more institutional than paternal. There was culpable overcrowding in dormitories or shared bedrooms, sometimes even shared beds; often no rooms for leisure activities, unappetising meals, no meals at all served on Sundays. At some hostels, the inmates were even *locked out* all day on Sundays, and those without friends' houses to visit could find themselves going to church three times a day, simply to have somewhere warm to sit. Generally speaking, the West End shops provided better staff accommodation than City and suburban shops, and their working hours were not quite so long, although 8 a.m. until 8 p.m., even later in summer, was not unusual. The Early Closing Association, formed in 1842, found its main opposition coming from the owners of low-price drapers and food shops in the suburbs, who did their briskest business after seven in the evening. By the mid 1860s some West End shops were closing at 2 p.m. on Saturdays, including Debenham & Freebody, Marshall & Snelgrove, Shoolbred and Lewis & Allenby. Swan & Edgar closed at 6 p.m. every evening in the winter, including Saturdays, at 7 p.m. in summer.

Arthur Lewis, son of the founder of Lewis & Allenby, was a man with musical and artistic interests, much travelled on the Continent. To a great extent he overcame the social disadvantage of being in retail trade. In 1859, A. J. Munby wrote in his diary of being invited with Walter Severn to a Bachelors' Ball at St James's Hall 'by a pleasant gentlemanly man named Lewis, the son and partner of the *mercer* in Regent Street! [Munby's italics and exclamation mark.] Lewis being modest and accomplished and having the wisdom not to be ashamed of his position, is much liked in good male society.' Note 'male society' – Munby did not expect him to mix with the wives and daughters of gentlemen. There is a remarkable resemblance of attitude in this diary entry to the passage in *Pride and Prejudice*, published forty-six years earlier, describing Mrs Bennett's brother, Mr Gardiner of Gracechurch Street in the City; 'Mr Gardiner was a sensible, gentlemanlike man, greatly superior to his sister as well by nature as by education. The Netherfield ladies would have had difficulty in believing that a man who lived by trade, and within view of his own warehouses, could have been so well bred and agreeable.' But Arthur Lewis, although he lived by trade, did not live within view of his own warehouses. He had a handsome residence called Moray Lodge on Campden Hill with grounds bordering those of Holland House, and he drove to the shop in his own carriage. He was one of the founders of the Arts Club whose membership included Charles Dickens, Lord Houghton and James Whistler; and at Moray Lodge he entertained celebrities of literary, artistic and stage circles. Thackeray, Trollope, George du Maurier, Leech, the Pre-Raphaelite painters and Henry Irving mingled there happily with Mr Poole the Savile Row tailor, and Mr Tattersall the horsedealer.

12 Kensington, Brompton and Chelsea

THE LAND between Knightsbridge and Kensington village was not entirely built over until after the Great Exhibition of 1851. The Exhibition brought the world and his wife to Hyde Park; and the profits from the Exhibition were used to buy the land between Kensington Gardens and Cromwell Road, on which were built museums, colleges and dignified premises for learned societies – a tribute to Prince Albert's encouragement of art and industry. Gore House, whose last tenant had been the gorgeous Lady Blessington, was rented for the duration of the Exhibition by the celebrated chef Alexis Soyer, who transformed the house and its beautiful garden into a sensationally expensive restaurant with sensationally avant-garde murals by Augustus Sala. Too expensive, too sensational for Victorian taste, it was not a success.

West of the new museum enclave, cultural shrine of mid-Victorian life, developers created a smart new residential quarter, for which Kensington High Street became the main shopping street. It was still a narrow, twisting road, lined with little dwelling houses, shops and no less than twenty-two public houses. One of the little shops belonged to Joseph Toms and was listed in the London Post Office Directory of 1854 as a 'Toy and Fancy Repository'. In 1862 Toms took Charles Derry into partnership, and so began the history of Derry & Toms department store. In their Kensington Improvement Scheme of 1867, the Metropolitan Board of Works decreed that the road be widened and 'A Handsome Range of Shop Property' be built on the south side. By 1870, the year in which John Baker started in Kensington, 'a noble roadway and 55 superior houses and shops' had been completed.

Meanwhile, the market-garden land that lay to the south of the museum country, between Cromwell Road and Brompton Road, had also been filled in with building – thus giving the little shops of Brompton village a new reservoir of moneyed customers. On the extreme eastern boundary of the village, near the top of Sloane Street, there was a little linen-draper's shop that had been opened by Benjamin Harvey in 1813. Harvey died the year before the Great Exhibition, leaving the business to his daughter Elizabeth with the recommendation that she take the silk buyer, Colonel Nichols, into partnership. The appearance of a colonel on the drapery scene is puzzling. Army and trade

were in totally distinct social strata. It could be that the silk buyer had joined the Volunteer Movement initiated in the 1840s when there was fear of invasion from France, and had achieved his rank through service to his country after work and on the short holidays then allowed to shop employees. The fact that the firm became named Harvey Nichols – not Harvey & Nichols – seems to support an assumption that Miss Harvey married the colonel. Certainly that would have made business life simpler in those days, when the owner lived over the shop – a marriage of convenience, if not of romance.

A little further west along the Brompton Road from Harvey Nichols, Henry Charles Harrod, a tea merchant of Eastcheap married to a pork butcher's daughter, bought in 1849 the little grocer's shop of P. H. Burden, whom he had befriended by allowing long credit. Burden had finally decided he must give up his unsuccessful business, and Harrod liked the idea of moving his family out from the City to the clean air of Brompton. Burden's home and shop were in a row of houses called Middle Queen's Buildings, some of whose front gardens had been built over with flat-roofed, single-storey shops. Harrod was nearly fifty at the time, and had no ambitions for the shop beyond making a modest living. He took on two assistants to serve in it, and himself carried on his wholesale tea trading in a small way.

Harrod's little grocer's shop began to extend along Brompton Road towards Knightsbridge in the 1880s.

Twelve years later, when his son Charles Digby Harrod was twenty, he handed over the shop to him on the understanding that it was not an inheritance but a business deal, to be paid for in instalments. Young Charles Digby was a hard worker, more ambitious than his father, and paid off the purchase price in three years. His success was partly due to the development of the neighbourhood following the Great Exhibition; but an important factor was undoubtedly his courage in determining to run the business on a strictly cash basis. Until then it had been customary for grocers to allow 'the nobility and gentry' to run up large accounts. Inevitably this made it necessary to charge high prices. Harrod offered, for cash, lower prices than his competitors, without lowering the quality of his merchandise. He also put an end to another custom, that of giving a commission to the servants on household orders – cook's perks as they were called.

There were usually more servants than family in the households of carriage folk, and their clothing was a not insignificant department of drapery. Footmen and coachmen's liveries were custom-made by tailors, and paid for by their employers, but women servants were usually expected to buy their own uniforms out of their meagre wages. In the mid-century there were shops in London and the larger cities called 'servants' bazaars'. The London Post Office Directory of 1859 lists two in Oxford Street: Archibald Thompson's at No. 252, and William Mills at No. 309. Woolland's in Knightsbridge, next door to Harvey Nichols, was opened in 1869 as a shop for servants; and Garrould's of Edgware Road, near the Marble Arch, also specialized in nurses' and maids' uniforms. In December 1877, an advertisement in the *West Middlesex Advertiser* invited ladies 'to recommend their Servants and Club Tickets to Joseph Cox, "the People's Draper" at Nos. 163 and 165 Marlborough Road, Brompton, being by consent the Cheapest House in the Neighbourhood for Drapery, Hosiery, Haberdashery, Flannels, Blankets, etc. etc.'

At Christmas time, season of good-will and generosity, many shops sold gift parcels for 'the deserving poor', and also for servants who ranked only one degree higher than the poor and were generally regarded as less deserving. A typical servants' gift parcel in one catalogue contained: '7 yards of double-width black merino, 2 yards of linen, 1 striped skirt, and 6 linen handkerchiefs'. The employer thus generously presented his maids with the materials to make their own uniforms, throwing in a few handkerchiefs to honour the festive spirit. Even the top servants of top households made their own uniforms. An assistant at Howell & James, who moved to Liberty's later, recalled: 'On many occasions it was my privilege to take and show a selection of 16-yard lengths of Grosgrain in various shades – emphatically *not* Liberty! – to Mrs Dodds, the lady housekeeper to the Princess of Wales at Marlborough House, to be distributed amongst the upper servants.'

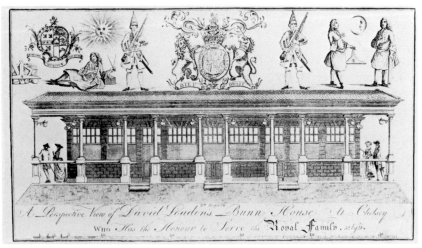

David Loudon's famous Bunn House in Chelsea, which 'Has the Honour to Serve the Royal Family'. Trade card c. 1730, signed Wm. Hogarth.

Chelsea, although no further from London than Kensington, maintained its separate identity much longer. Until the King's private road from Whitehall Palace to Hampton Court was opened to public traffic in 1830, Church Lane was the only way into Chelsea by stage coach: the White Horse, opposite Chelsea Old Church, was the posting house. But one could reach Chelsea by river, and the idea of living in a riverside village was attractive to artists, poets and literary men. There was also a sprinkling of aristocracy in elegant seventeenth- and eighteenth-century terraces. With Ranelagh for music, masquerades, merry-making and mild debauchery, with Cremorne for less mild debauchery, Chelsea drew from London pleasure-seekers of every high and low degree. But by the beginning of the nineteenth century, the aristocrats and other prosperous residents had decided that Chelsea was no longer fashionable. Most of them moved away to Mayfair, or to Hans Town. The houses they left behind them in Chelsea were let to middle-class tenants, or taken over for lodging houses. Terraces of smaller houses were built to accommodate professional families moving out from the City, or newcomers from the provinces.

Among the newcomers were Mr and Mrs Thomas Carlyle from Scotland, who took up residence at 24 Cheyne Row in 1834. From Thea Holme's *Chelsea*, we learn that the Carlyles found they were able to do nearly all their shopping locally: in Cheyne Walk there was an ironmonger, a greengrocer and a chemist called Allson from whom Thomas bought his blue pills and castor oil. There was a tobacconist in the King's Road, and another in Church Street, both of whom he patronized for his cigars. There was also a hosier and a haberdasher in Church Street. In Lombard Street, past the church, there was a fishmonger, and fresh fish could also be bought at the wharfs, straight from the fishermen's boats. The Carlyles had their milk delivered by local dairymen, first Mr Brimblecombe, then Mr Shakespear, both of whom milked their own cows on the premises; sometimes, the Carlyles suspected, it was also watered on the premises. They were critical of the eggs supplied by the Egg and Butter Merchant, and Jane sent for eggs from Scotland which, not surprisingly, were apt to arrive 'all in a state of *mush*'. Bread was delivered to the door, and on winter Sundays the muffin man's bell heralded his appearance in Cheyne Row with his tray on his head. The famous 'Bunn House at the King's Arms at Chelsey', on the corner of Grosvenor Row, was pulled down four years after the Carlyles came to Chelsea. It had been kept from the seventeenth century by four generations of the Hand family, and then became David Loudon's Bunn House. His trade-card, *c.* 1730, carried the signature Wm. Hogarth.

Before the King's Road was opened to public traffic, there were only a few cottages with little front gardens along it, and one or two larger houses standing back in their own grounds. Even after the road became public, new building was mostly confined to small houses and little shops supplying basic household needs: a butcher's shop, a dairy, one or two grocers and a bakery called Beeton's. But after the mid-century, one of the streets leading north off the King's Road became quite well known for fashion goods. This was Marlborough Road, now named Draycott Avenue. Peter Jones – a Welshman who had been an assistant in several shops, including that of Stagg & Mantle, a drapery of some renown in Leicester Square – in 1871 rented two houses in Marlborough Road and knocked them into one shop. A year later the building collapsed, killing his apprentice and burying his wife (temporarily) in the rubble. Despite this dramatic setback, Jones rebuilt; and his business then prospered to such an extent (perhaps thanks to the publicity from the disaster) that he was able by 1877 to rent Nos. 4 and 6 King's Road, near the junction with Sloane Square, premises previously occupied by Lambe Brothers, linen drapers. Here he was in a strategic position to attract both Hans Town residents and the aristocracy of Belgravia. He even had the delirious delight of supplying hats to Buckingham Palace for the royal children. Within seven years he had 150 employees and had taken over two more houses; during the next ten years he acquired a further ten, and had rebuilt the whole row as one shop of five storeys, crowned by a turret; and, according to *The Builder*, his premises 'were the first of their character to be lighted with electricity'.

Such rapid expansion indicates that Peter Jones was a man of industry and drive. He was also a good master, providing more amenities for his staff than were usual at the time – a library, a billiard room, a piano; and, according to Mrs Florence Nye, who was apprenticed to the millinery department in the early 'eighties (and who is quoted by Thea Holme), the food was very good. The vanmen lived in a house beside the stables where eighteen horses were kept to make two deliveries daily, including Saturdays. They started work at seven a.m., cleaning harness and vans, grooming horses, then worked until nine p.m., when the horses were fed and stabled. On Sundays they went twice to the stables to look after the horses. Everyone, according to Mrs Nye, was happy working for Peter Jones; but when the master fell ill in 1903 and was no longer at the helm, the business changed direction. Quality was no longer the chief consideration. There were frequent 'special offers' of cheap job-lots and bought-in bankrupt stock. The best customers began to go elsewhere. A year after Peter Jones's death in 1905, his widow sold out to John Lewis of Oxford Street, who, motivated by the thrift that had made his own business so profitable, walked from Oxford Street to Sloane Square with the purchase price of £22,500 in banknotes in his pocket.

John Lewis had started his London career as a silk buyer at Peter Robinson's, and when he set up on his own in 1864 it was a bold purchase of a job lot of silks that set his ball rolling. From then on he built up his business by 'buying cheap and selling cheap'. Hard on his staff, he was not all that cordial to his customers and was known to have snatched a cigar from the mouth of one gentleman in his shop. But Lewis's autocratic crustiness and cheese-paring policies were less successful in Sloane Square than in Oxford Street. After eight years, during which Peter Jones failed to make a profit, he handed over total control of the ailing shop to his elder son, Spedan Lewis, who had long been a thorn in his father's flesh because of his democratic ideas. Spedan then, as Chairman of Peter Jones, was at last able to put into practice some of his theories about staff involvement and profit sharing. Thus the seeds of the John Lewis Partnership, now grown to a many-branched organization, were originally sown at Peter Jones in Sloane Square.

Peter Jones of Sloane Square: ground floor and gallery
(with Refreshment area at right, next to Patent
Medicines) in 1890 (right) and the new building erected
before the turn of the century (above). After Peter Jones
died, the business was sold to John Lewis, whose Oxford
Street shop (below, late 1880s) was rebuilt in 1895 –
Lewis's original little shop of 1864 was sited where the
'N' and the 'L' of the facia are fixed.

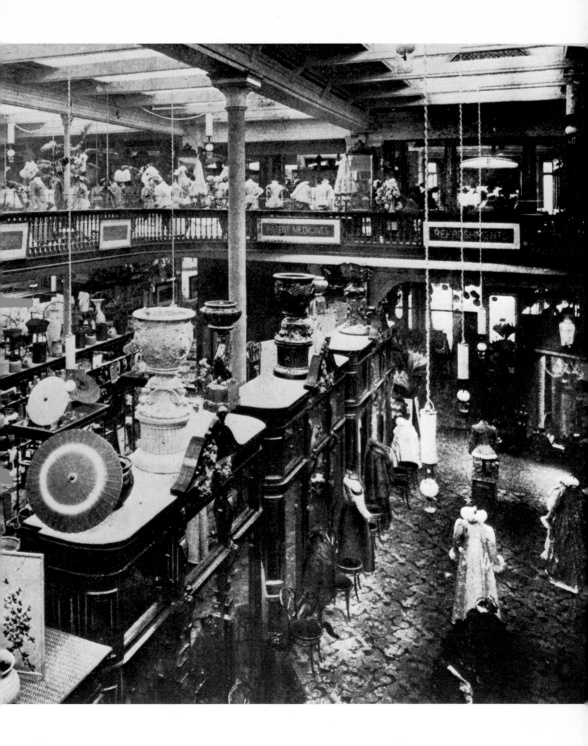

13 Growth of department stores

*Own brand trading: the
'Special Smoking Mixture' of
the Army & Navy Stores.*

*Opposite: Peter Robinson's
rapid growth had by 1891
covered sites on Oxford Street,
Regent Street, Great Portland
Street, Argyll Street and
Market Place.*

THE LAND north of Hyde Park beyond Tyburn toll-gate had remained rural all through the first quarter of the nineteenth century. Bayswater was described in a guide-book of 1820 as 'a small hamlet in the parish of Paddington, Middlesex, one mile West from London'. The Rev. J. Richardson wrote of it in his *Recollections*: 'The place was a blank in the improvements of London for years after other suburbs had been built upon.' In the 1820s, a little sporadic development broke out along the high road to Oxford, facing Hyde Park; and when planners of residential property moved in, this length of the high road as far as Notting Hill was named Bayswater Road. Fine family houses were built upon it, pompous and porticoed. They had delightful views over the Park, where sheep and cows still grazed in summer, and where the children, escorted by nannies and nursemaids, could be given their daily airing. To the rear of the houses, land lay open to the village of Paddington, although before long the fields were covered by residential streets, terraces and squares.

Westbourne Grove, where William Whiteley opened his shop in 1863, was not one of these handsome new streets. It was a rural road lined by little cottages with front gardens, as in a country town or village. In effect, it served as the northern boundary to the fashionable new suburb, sealing it off from waste land and ramshackle property to the north. The cottages were pulled down and replaced with houses suitable for middle-class tenants and shops to serve the district. Unfortunately for the shopkeepers, the 'carriage folk' of the grander terraces and squares showed no inclination to shop in Westbourne Grove: they drove to Oxford Street, Regent Street and Bond Street. Some who had moved from the now unfashionable Bloomsbury remained faithful to Shoolbred's in Tottenham Court Road, who made great efforts to retain the loyalty of their customers when they moved westwards. As a result, business was anything but brisk in Westbourne Grove, and it became known in the trade as Bankruptcy Avenue. William Whiteley was taking a big gamble in starting there.

He had indeed hesitated, thinking seriously of Upper Street, Islington. Islington village had become a suburb, well served by horse omnibuses – a local directory of 1863 advertised 'omnibuses to and from

Peter Robinson, 1891.

216 TO 228 OXFORD ST. & 1 TO 9 GT. PORTLAND ST.

256 TO 262 REGENT ST.

INTERIOR OXFORD ST.

INTERIOR REGENT ST.

CARRIAGE ENTRANCE, 19 TO 21 ARGYLE ST.

21 TO 24 MARKET PLACE.

NEW BUILDINGS, 204 TO 212 OXFORD ST. ERECTED 1890-1891.

228 REGENT ST.

282 TO 286 REGENT ST.

MR. PETER ROBINSON'S BUSINESS PREMISES, OXFORD STREET AND REGENT STREET, LONDON.

139

all parts every 5 minutes at a flat rate of 4d'. Architecturally pleasing squares and terraces attracted middle-class families seeking healthy air above the City, and the increasing purchasing power of these classes in Victoria's reign was reflected in the increasing prosperity of the local tradesmen. In Upper Street, the drapery shop of T. R. Roberts was expanding swiftly into a department store, and he had an equally go-ahead rival in Rackstraw's. It was not only the residents of Islington, Canonbury, Holloway and Highbury that they served; people came by omnibus from further afield, and the reputation of Upper Street shops even attracted carriage trade from the West End. By one of the inexplicable quirks of fashionable patronage, Upper Street gained a particular reputation for underclothes, and was thus a favoured place for brides to come with their mammas to buy their trousseaux. Mr R. Allin, of 73 Upper Street and 464 Kingsland Road, specialized in handmade underclothing, as did E. Avis, who offered also a very special speciality in his 'Spatula Corsets'.

Nevertheless, Whiteley made a wise decision in choosing Westbourne Grove instead of Upper Street, for the carriage trade drifted away from Islington before the end of the nineteenth century, leaving only Mr and Mrs Pooter and their like to patronize the local shops. Even the Pooters – immortal suburban characters of George and Weedon Grossmith's *Diary of a Nobody* – preferred to go to the West End for special purchases. It was at Shoolbred's in Tottenham Court Road that Carrie bought her three-and-sixpenny white fan; and it was Liberty silk that made the bows she arranged at the corners of their enlarged and tinted photographs. When Mr Pooter was promoted at the office, he told her: 'At last you shall have that little costume that you saw at Peter Robinson's so cheap.' The handkerchiefs she bought for him locally at the Holloway Road Bon Marché sale were *not* a good buy. They lost their colour in the wash. The Pooters' proudest possession, the cottage piano they bought 'on the three year system', came from Collard & Collard of Bond Street, no less.

Mary Vivien Thomas, who lived in Canonbury in the 1870s, makes no mention at all of Canonbury or Islington shops in her autobiography *A London Family*. She relates that she often went with her mother by bus to Shoolbred's or to Peter Robinson's: 'A morning's shopping was all we could manage for one day, for, strange as it seems now, the big shops had no restaurants, no rest-rooms, no conveniences for toilet, however dire one's need.' It was not until 1884 that the Ladies' Lavatory Company opened its first establishment at Oxford Circus, most conveniently near Peter Robinson's. But even if it had been there, Mrs Thomas and her daughter's need would have had to have been dire indeed for them to resort to it, since 'ladies feared to be seen entering'. On the other hand, if they had been shopping in Kensington, they would have found relief from all anxiety in the ultra-modern department store of Seaman Little & Co., built on the newly widened High Street in 1870. This progressive firm's bright new ideas included 'handsomely appointed lavatories for customers' convenience situated beyond the three perfectly equipped fitting rooms for dressmaking, millinery, etc.' On the floor above were dressmaking workrooms where over ninety hands were employed; and at the top of the building was a large kitchen

Westbourne Grove: afternoon shopping in 1884.

'from which the food descends by lift to the staff dining-room in the basement'. It must have been thought quite revolutionary to have a kitchen on the top floor; but contemporary planning evidently had not advanced so far as to have the dining-room alongside. Apart from the ninety workroom hands, the firm employed over one hundred and fifty assistants, all living in, and the size of this one firm gives some indication of the popularity Kensington High Street was acquiring as a shopping street. Derry & Toms by this time owned seven shops in a row, with a separate shop as a mourning department.

One of the factors that influenced Whiteley's choice of Westbourne Grove was that London's first Underground Railway, the Metropolitan, was to be opened in 1863. It was to run from Farringdon Street in the City to Bishop's Road, serving the Great Western Railway terminus at Paddington. Bishop's Road station was only a short walk from Westbourne Grove. The omnibus service, also, was good – the Great Exhibition, with its invasion of visitors to London, had brought about an omnibus boom. Whiteley had the foresight to realize that the new mobility and purchasing power of middle-class shoppers would bring him greater profits than the patronage of the carriage trade. He was not a man of impulse but of purpose, and planned every step he took with the greatest care. Apprenticed when he was seventeen to Harnew and Glover, the largest drapery shop in Wakefield, on the very day his indentures expired he left Wakefield and set himself systematically to study every aspect of London's drapery trade. He spent fifteen months behind the counter at R. Willey & Co. of Ludgate Street, then moved to the great wholesale house of Morrison & Dillon. Next he worked with specialists in the ribbon trade, then made one more move to wholesalers Bradbury, Greatorex, & Beall. While he worked and studied he saved, so that when he opened his first little shop in Westbourne Grove selling ribbons, lace and fancy goods, he had sufficient capital to engage two young lady assistants.

His next step was to marry one of the young ladies, so assuring himself of her unpaid labour twenty-four hours a day instead of the twelve to fourteen which were then normal shop working hours. Within a year he had fifteen assistants apart from his wife, plus a cashier and two errand boys – a staff far beyond the average for the neighbourhood. Three more years and he had extended into silks, linens, mantles, drapery, millinery, ladies' outfitting, jewellery, furs, umbrellas, and artificial flowers. One of his assistants was an enthusiastic young man called John Barker.

John Barker had worked his way up in the trade the hard way, like Whiteley himself. Born in 1840 in Maidstone and apprenticed to a local draper before he was thirteen, he became a junior assistant in a Folkestone shop on completing his indentures, and then joined a Dover draper. At eighteen he came to London to take a post at Spencer, Turner & Boldero of Lisson Grove, drapers and furnishers, founded in 1840. Lisson Grove was then a good shopping street. Although technically in the parish of Paddington, it served St Marylebone, which was then at the height of its favour as a residential quarter before the decline of

From Maidstone draper's apprentice to Sir John Barker, MP for Penryn and Falmouth, lionized in the Society magazine Vanity Fair. *His store was 'devoted to the supply of all classes of goods at the lowest possible prices'.*

population living in the borough, as distinct from working in it, began in the 1870s. John Barker, in leaving Lisson Grove to join Whiteley, was abandoning a fashionable quarter where business was about to decline, for another where fashionable trade was beginning to develop. Spencer, Turner & Boldero themselves, before the end of the century, opened branches in Devonshire Street and Duke Street, to counterbalance the deterioration of Lisson Grove.

Whiteley made John Barker a department manager within a few years, with a salary of £300 a year. He soon demanded more, and Whiteley said he would double his salary if he doubled the firm's turnover in the next year. The turnover was doubled, and so was the department manager's salary. As Whiteley continued to buy more adjacent properties and add more departments, John Barker asked to be taken into partnership. This was refused, but Whiteley offered to make his salary £1,000. The year was 1870, and such a salary was unheard of for a drapery employee. But Barker wanted directorial power as well, for he had many ideas he wanted to put into practice. So he turned his back on Whiteley and Westbourne Grove and made for Kensington High Street, which he rightly sensed had a great shopping future.

After Barker's departure, Whiteley branched out far beyond traditional drapery lines. This was greatly resented by local shopkeepers, who considered it unfair trading for a draper to sell groceries and meat, ironmongery and books, to go into the house agency business and outside catering, to have a hairdressing saloon, dry-cleaning and laundry services. The only service that it was traditional for a draper to offer, beyond drapery, was funeral undertaking. This, it hardly needs saying,

143

Whiteley undertook. He was now calling himself the Universal Provider, and naturally had to offer the ultimate provision to his customers. It was probably the influence of local publicans that prevented Whiteley from being granted a licence for his restaurant, although the Paddington magistrate gave a different reason. Remarking that 'Mr. Whiteley had got enough irons in the fire already', he refused it 'in the interests of morality. . . . Many of Mr. Whiteley's customers might be ladies, or females dressed to represent them, and the place might be made a place of assignation.'

Whiteley's success drew other retailers to Bayswater, and the 1887 edition of *Modern London* described Westbourne Grove as *The Bond Street of the West*, with an ecstatic eulogy of Whiteley's:

Depot, emporium, bazaar, warehouse – none of these seem to possess the slightest descriptive power. Whiteley's is an immense symposium of the arts and industries of the nation and of the world; a grand review of everything that goes to make life worth living passing in seemingly endless array before critical but bewildered humanity; an international exhibition of the resources and products of the earth and air, flood and field.

One of the newcomers drawn into the orbit of Whiteley's wondrous emporium was Mr Bradley, who opened in 1870 the Arctic Fur Store in Chepstow Place, leading off Westbourne Grove. He was a direct importer of raw skins, had a flair for designing magnificent fur coats, and claimed to be the first furrier to have cold air chambers for storing customers' furs in the summer. Later, while still maintaining its supremacy with furs, Bradley's became one of London's leading tailoring and dressmaking houses. Its workrooms, showrooms and eighty-six fitting rooms covered an area of nearly six acres. The firm was run by members of the Bradley family until 1953, when it was acquired by Debenham & Freebody.

Tom Ponting was the next to make his mark in Bayswater. He was one of four Ponting brothers from Gloucester who came to London in 1873. The other three started in Kensington High Street. Also in 1873, a Welshman named William Owen opened his 'Bayswater Trimming Shop' just opposite Whiteley's. Soon the trimmings were supplemented with gloves and 'fancy goods'. In less than ten years he had bought fifteen shops in Hatherley Grove, two in Westbourne Grove, and had 350 employees. It would seem from an account in *Modern London* of his 'immense emporium' that Owen concentrated more on fashion than did Whiteley:

Up a particularly handsome staircase in American walnut of the most artistic design, is the main showroom for gowns and millinery, probably unsurpassed in size and elegance of appointment by any similar exhibition salon in London. The arts of the skilled *modiste* stand here exemplified in all their highest phases . . . velvets and velveteens, crapes and mourning goods, laces, hosiery, wools, art needlework, costume clothes, underclothing, corsets, baby linen, straws, flowers, feathers, and dressing-gowns.

Ponting's of Kensington High Street at its zenith in 1913.

William Owen prided himself upon his delivery service. It was not as far reaching as Whiteley's, which penetrated a radius of twenty-five miles

round London, with 320 horses and 145 vehicles. But Owen's vans were prodigiously smart, and his elegant horses enjoyed 'the only stables in London, with the exception of Tattersalls, that have patent mangers divided into apartments for the reception of hay and other sorts of provender. . . . The horses are all of the best, and everything that can add to their comfort is done.' The horses' board and lodging sounds far superior to anything Owen's shop assistants are likely to have experienced in their hostels, although he may have been one of the less culpable employers in this respect.

William Whiteley was a hard, mean master. He housed his male employees in big dormitories at one end of his Queen's Road premises, and his female employees in lodgings in Hatherley Grove and Westbourne Grove Terrace. Girls slept two or three to a bedroom, which had to serve as their sitting-room also, although no chairs were provided. On Sundays the rooms had to be vacated all day, whether or not a girl had anywhere to go. Meals, which were in communal dining-rooms in the basement of Whiteley's shops, were not served on the Sabbath. There was a list of 176 trivial rules, and fines were imposed for breaking any of them. Rules and fines were quite usual in the big shops of the day, but at Whiteley's a daily list of offenders was pinned on a board; and the fines did not go to any charity or staff benefit fund, but straight into Mr Whiteley's pocket. On joining the firm, each employee had to sign a form stating that no notice was required on either side – he or she could be dismissed or could leave (without a reference, of course) at a moment's notice.

On the credit side it was said that meals at Whiteley's were more adequate – or less inadequate – than those provided by most other shops. But the very short break allowed in which to eat them meant they could neither be enjoyed nor well digested. Another credit was that Whiteley did actively encourage out-of-shop activities, forming an athletic club, rowing club, 'musical union', choral society and a dramatic society. He can scarcely be credited with providing the staff library, since employees had sixpence deducted every month from their wages to pay for the books. Sixpence a month was also deducted for shoe-cleaning, and another sixpence for the 'house doctor', whether you were ill or not.

Meanwhile, in the Strand a new kind of retail shop, a co-operative, was creating interest. Co-operative retailing originated in Rochdale during the Hungry Forties and was an entirely working-class movement in the provinces. But in 1864 a group of clerks in the London General Post Office clubbed together to buy a chest of tea, thereby saving themselves ninepence in the pound. Soon they were buying wholesale groceries of all kinds, and in 1866 they named their operation the Civil Service Supply Association. Two years later they opened a shop in the Strand retailing a wide range of clothing, household linen and hardware, supplied by affiliated private traders; and by 1870 the store offered under one roof practically all the necessities of life that people were accustomed to buy in numerous different shops.

One year later, in 1871, a small group of officers of the armed forces, indignant at the price of wine (a bottle of good port cost two shillings!),

The shop assistant as a 'Free Englishman', surrounded by the rules of his master. Ushered into the forbidding presence of William Whiteley, the applicant was eyed disapprovingly: 'Good morning, young man' (spoken as if through his nose), 'I have vacancies in my linen, furnishing, oriental, dress and country order departments – supposing I was to engage you . . .'

determined to reduce the cost of living by ordering wine by the case at wholesale prices. How pleasingly appropriate it is that the Civil Service Stores started with a chest of tea, and the Army & Navy Stores with a case of wine. The following year, the officers opened a retail shop in Victoria Street. This was a new street, part of the mid-Victorian road improvement scheme for London, and was driven through acres of slums from Westminster Abbey to Victoria Station. Without architectural unity, it had nothing to commend it aesthetically. It was not a residential street, nor yet a shopping street. If anything it was a business street, unlovely and unloved. Nevertheless, the Army & Navy Co-operative Society took half a building occupied by Joseph and John Vickers & Company. The rents in fashionable streets were too high for the Society, and in any case there was no need to attract customers in the usual way. On the contrary, the Stores were a 'closed shop' in the sense that only members could shop there.

Membership was restricted to officers and non-commissioned officers, their families and friends introduced by them, together with officials of various service organizations and clubs. The subscription was five shillings for the first year, then half-a-crown annually. There were no display windows and from the outside the stores looked more like a club than a shop. Indeed, for many of its members it served as a club, particularly appreciated by women, who then had no clubs of their own. There were reading rooms with all the newspapers, writing rooms, cloakrooms; you could meet friends in the Refreshment Room for breakfast (9.15 to 11 a.m.) or for the two-shilling *table d'hôte* luncheon, no gratuities. The salesmen and doormen were like club servants,

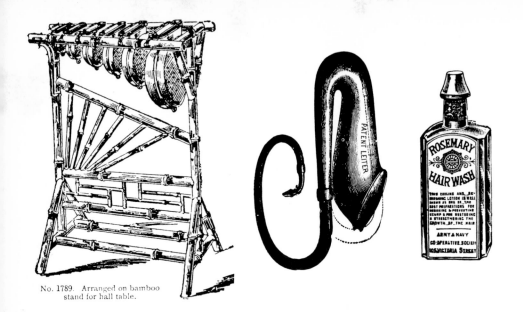

No. 1789. Arranged on bamboo
stand for hall table.

infallible in recognizing members and addressing them by name. Even if
you had been abroad for years and years, you would be welcomed
warmly by name. When you were far from England, the great
clothbound annual catalogue kept you in touch with 'home' – was,
indeed, a very tangible touch of 'home'. Through it, you could order
absolutely everything, from dinner gongs to laxatives, from tents,
trunks and lawn-mowers, to ear-trumpets, trusses and hair-restorers.

Soon the Army & Navy brought down prices still lower by having its
own factories to make confectionery and groceries, bread, cigars and
cigarettes, shirts and leather goods, watches, saddlery, guns, golf clubs.
It executed carpentry, printing, engraving, taxidermy; it produced
drugs and distilled perfumes, and had a service 'devoted to the ingenious
and effective cleaning of sponges, a great feature of the Society'. Less
intimate services included house removals and warehousing, auction
rooms, estate agency, repairs and decorations, catering. As it was in the
beginning and is now, wine was a very important part of the business.
The Society shipped, bottled and stored most of the wines it sold. Port
and sherry were blended in huge vats, still in the Army & Navy cellars,
made of Baltic oak which has been unobtainable since the Russian
Revolution. Army & Navy blends of whisky were 'in strengths which
are of a much higher degree than obtain in proprietary brands so
extensively and expensively advertised'.

Another landmark in the history of retailing, vastly different from the
Army & Navy Stores, was built in 1876. This was the Bon Marché
department store in Brixton, the first in the London area to be *built* as a
store instead of starting as a small shop and growing by the acquisition
of adjacent property. The Bon Marché was a colossal gamble. Its sole
backer was James Smith, a printer by trade and proprietor of the
Sportsman, who had pulled off a double by winning the Cesarewitch and
the Cambridgeshire Stakes. The *Builder* magazine hailed the Bon Marché

A Brixton tram advertises the attractions of a Bon Marché sale in 1894 (above) *– and the store as it was in the 1960s* (below).

as 'a novelty in market accommodation in the metropolis, embracing the sale of almost every imaginable article in food, furniture and dress, under one management, the whole of the employees residing on the premises'. The assistants' dining-room could hold 300 at a sitting, which gives an idea of the size of the whole building.

Trading was to be strictly on a cash basis, and local shopkeepers, who dared not offend their old customers by refusing credit, were alarmed at the prospect of their prices being undercut. One of them, anticipating total ruin, committed suicide – unnecessarily, as it turned out, since the Bon Marché did not flourish. Mr Smith was in the bankruptcy court within fifteen years of its opening. No doubt he had overestimated the trading prospects of the district; but the main reason for his failure was probably his total lack of experience in retailing. All successful shopkeepers of the nineteenth century learned their trade from apprenticeship upwards. The Bon Marché was salvaged by five experienced retailers, who turned it into a public company in 1892 and 'traded it up' to Kensington department store standards – well, not quite Kensington, but it did have fitted carpets in all departments. Customers now came to it from the nearby, but socially superior suburbs of Clapham and Streatham, where there were large houses in big gardens with stabling and greenhouses.

William Edgar, founder of Swan & Edgar, bought a handsome property at Clapham called Eagle House, from where his daughter was triumphantly married to a baronet. The retired draper in Mrs Braddon's novel *The Rose of Life* also lived in Clapham and was able to give his daughter £30,000 as her marriage portion. Mrs Braddon was a skilful analyst of the nuances of class:

Mr. Dowden's hot-houses were the draper's chief pride. He had more glass than his partner Plowden, and prettier daughters; but the Plowdens, who lived in Bayswater, gave themselves more airs, and cultivated professional society. The Dowdens revolved in a circle of other shopkeepers and their families, keeping company with jewellery and fur, with silver and plated goods, with books and stationery, but not with butcher's meat, pastry, or poultry.

As more and smaller houses were built in Clapham, the richer residents moved further out. William Edgar's son, when he inherited Swan & Edgar at his father's death, moved to Kingston Hill and rode to town on horseback. In Mrs Braddon's novel, the Dowden daughters grew to be ashamed of Clapham:

'It's a pity the tide of fashion has ebbed away from Clapham Park,' said Mr. Dowden.
'Oh, father, Clapham Park was never fashionable,' Sally murmured.
'What, not when the Gaylords and the Trowmongers, and the Hartlepools all had houses here!', protested her father, naming three well-known firms in Regent Street and Piccadilly. 'Your mother and I used to dine out three or four times a week in the season, and some of the finest turn-outs in Hyde Park came from Clapham.'

Of those retailers who made their homes to the north of London, James Marshall, founder of Marshall & Snelgrove, was almost certainly

the earliest to do so in the grand style. In 1859 he bought Goldbeater Farm at Mill Hill with a thousand acres. When the Midland Railway was constructed to pass through his estate, Marshall was allowed to choose the site of Mill Hill Station, and had the right to stop any express train to suit his convenience. He gave staff garden parties and cricket matches, and his elder son, James C. Marshall, founded the Linen & Woollen Drapers Cottage Homes for retired members of the trade, giving the land from the Goldbeater Estate and financing much of the building. In the 1880s, John Lewis built a commanding residence with a look-out turret in four acres of grounds overlooking Hampstead Heath; and in the early 1890s, John Barker bought The Grange, Bishop's Stortford, with 300 acres on which he bred Syrian sheep and polo ponies. Meanwhile, in Buckinghamshire Arthur Liberty had taken Lee Manor near Chesham and was soon landowner of some 3,000 acres. After the turn of the century, he became High Sheriff of Buckinghamshire, Deputy Lieutenant of the County, was knighted and made a Freeman of the City of London. Thus the prestige and prosperity of London's famous department stores was reflected in the life-style of their founders.

The first of the *ABC* tea-shops
opened in *1880* and by the end of
the century, as this sketch
indicates, they had become
popular with all kinds of office
workers. The first Lyons tea shop
opened in Piccadilly in *1894* on
the site to the far right of this
photograph, c. *1880*.

14 Victorian zenith –
new adventures in retailing

From the Liberty's Silks *catalogue,* c. *1896.*

WITH THE INCREASING speed and frequency of main-line trains and the introduction of day-return tickets, West End shops drew customers from far afield. Even in the 1870s Lady Jebb used to go to London for a day's shopping from Cambridge, 54 miles each way, as did her niece Maud Darwin in the next decade. Others travelled even longer distances. In 1886 the *Lady's World* wrote: 'Now that the train service is so perfect between London and Bath, it is quite possible to spend a day in town and return to Bath the same evening. This is no small advantage when you have a day's shopping to get through, or winter gowns and mantles to be tried on at your favourite London modiste's.'

Naturally day-shoppers were most attracted to the large stores where there were restaurants and cloakrooms. Until the ABC tea shops started in 1880, there was nowhere for young women or married ladies to have a meal by themselves or to meet friends outside their own homes. The ABCs were a blessing to the new professional and business women; indeed, Roger Fulford in *Votes for Women* contends that the tea shop was an integral part of the Women's Suffrage Movement. The first Lyons' Tea Shop opened in Piccadilly in 1894. But more leisured ladies required more gracious surroundings; and these the department stores provided. Soft carpets and music (usually a ladies' string quartet), dainty waitresses and pretty china, gossip with a woman friend, made luncheon and afternoon tea delightful interludes in the day's shopping. Moreover, and this was part of the plot, they put one in the mood to buy.

For country customers who could only visit London rarely or not at all, the leading stores had postal services. Catalogues were sent out regularly, from which a selection of clothes could be ordered on approval. When they arrived, you made your choice and returned the rest. In 1888 Marshall & Snelgrove's Country Rooms employed over a hundred clerks and accountants – about a thousand letters were received daily – and there were Examining Rooms where each order was inspected before dispatch. At this time Marshall & Snelgrove employed altogether 2,000 workers, of whom 700 boarded on the premises, with library and sitting rooms, smoking rooms, committee room, reading rooms. Their old premises, made up of a conglomeration of houses, had been replaced in 1876 by a five-storey building in French château style, occupying a complete island site. The building remains today.

HAPPY THOUGHT.

Nurse. "WELL, MASTER TOM, AND SO THE TWINS ARE GOING TO BE CHRISTENED TO-MORROW. WHAT SHALL WE CALL THEM?"
Tom (mindful of his Mother's fashionable proclivities). "IF WE WANT TO PLEASE MAMMA, WE'D BETTER CALL THEM *MARSHALL AND SNELGROVE!*"

Marshall & Snelgrove's imposing Oxford Street emporium, built in 1876, brought the store a fashionable reputation worthy of comment by Punch *in the following year.*

Another development during the last three decades of the nineteenth century was the emergence of shops catering for the individual tastes and enthusiasms of specific groups of people. For example, Liberty's of Regent Street was born out of Arthur Lasenby Liberty's involvement with the aesthetic movement, in which oriental silks, furnishings, pottery and artwork played an influential part. Liberty, when a nineteen-year-old employee at Farmer & Rogers' Great Shawl & Cloak Emporium in Regent Street, had visited the International Exhibition of 1862 which was held on the site of Gore House, later covered by the Albert Hall. It was at this exhibition that the arts and crafts of Japan (for over two centuries a closed civilization) were first shown to the Western world, and they created intense excitement in artistic circles. Liberty was so entranced that he persuaded his employers to buy all the Japanese exhibits available when the Exhibition was over. This they did, making them the nucleus of an Oriental Bazaar next door to their main shop. As manager of the Bazaar, Liberty met most of the leading designers, architects and painters of the day, and he made friends with the Pre-Raphaelite artists who enthused over the subtly coloured silks and the blue-and-white Oriental china.

After thirteen years, during which Liberty made the Oriental Bazaar the most profitable part of Farmer & Rogers' business, he asked to be taken into partnership. When this was refused, he was encouraged by his artist friends to start on his own in premises on the other side of Regent Street. It was only half a shop that he acquired, No. 218A, but he grandly called it East India House. He filled his window with the soft-draping Oriental silks that were fast becoming a cult of aesthetic ladies living in what *Punch* called Passionate Brompton. In 1884 he opened dressmaking workrooms, where Liberty gowns were designed that were totally *hors*

de la mode set by Paris. Instead of having tight-fitting bodices and
prominent rear bustles, as was then the fashion, they were loose and free-
flowing, following the lines of Grecian draperies. Isadora Duncan and
Ellen Terry were among those who became Liberty's most devoted
customers.

The Liberty furnishing department, regarded as a trendsetter,
advanced from the Japanese craze to a mode for all things Moorish.
Arab smoking rooms were designed for rich European clients, featuring
hanging mosque lamps, brass repoussé incense burners, lattice-work
screens, eastern rugs, intricately carved furniture. An early contract
executed by Liberty's design studio was for a Moorish music room in the
Marquess of Aberdeen's house in Grosvenor Square. Arthur Liberty
himself was neither a designer nor a craftsman, but he had an instinct for
the fashionable taste of tomorrow, and might be called an impresario of
the decorative arts. Farmer & Rogers made a fatal mistake in refusing to
take him into partnership, for their business fell away sharply after his
departure and closed down within five years. Their premises were taken
over by the business next door: Butterick's Paper Patterns, which had
come to Regent Street from America in 1873.

A totally different kind of shop, catering for totally different
enthusiasms, also had its conception at the Exhibition of 1862. One of
the stands was that of John Lillywhite, exhibiting 'articles connected
with cricket'. So much interest was shown in his stand by the general
public that the Lillywhite family (famous cricketers all) were encouraged
to start a retail shop at 31 Haymarket the following year. The opening of
this first specialist sports shop coincided with the start of a period of
immense enthusiasm for new sports. There was the fashionable craze for
croquet, the introduction of lawn tennis, the elegant country-house

Tailormade costumes of 1902. The 'lady's rinking outfit', c. 1910, is worn with roller skates and a large velvet toque.

sport of archery. The first ladies' golf club was opened in 1867, boldly at St Andrews. There was the roller-skating mania of the 'eighties, and the fashion for bicycling that took over in the 'nineties. Before the end of the century, the British had pioneered Scandinavian skiing as a sport in Switzerland. All these sports required their special equipment, and Lillywhite's became *the* place to get it. The shop, requiring more space, soon moved to its present premises in the Criterion building on Piccadilly Circus.

The pursuit of the exclusive and expensive pleasure of yachting was tailored by John Morgan of West Cowes, who opened a London branch in 1883, and by Gieves of Old Bond Street, established in 1785, who had been Lord Nelson's tailors. For Queen Victoria they designed a 'boat cloak' lined with scarlet, virtually the same as an admiral's cloak; and they made another for Queen Elizabeth II to wear on the naval barge taking her to dine with the Lords of the Admiralty at Greenwich after her coronation. She wore it again when escorted to dine on HMS *Ark Royal* during her Silver Jubilee review of the Fleet. Gieves have now joined forces with Hawkes, established in 1771 at 1 Savile Row – an appropriate alliance for Nelson's tailors, since Hawkes are livery and military tailors to HM the Queen, and their roll-call of famous clients includes the Duke of Wellington.

The tailormade costume that Victorian ladies wore for yachting became, by the 1880s, the prevailing fashion for everyday wear. It was unusual for a vogue to originate in England, not France, but after the fall of the Second Empire in 1870, Englishwomen no longer went to Paris for their clothes. Leading London 'Court Dressmakers' began to acquire a status akin to that of Parisian couture houses, setting styles instead of slavishly following those set by Paris. London men's tailors had always been superior to French tailors, and their skill was now turned to ladies' clothes. The tailormade costume reflected the personality of the 'New Woman', who was primarily an English species. It was hardly a liberating costume, with its stiff-collared shirt-blouse and tie, tight petersham-belted waist, skirt to the ground. But there was an efficient atmosphere about it, which expressed the mood of the young women who were determined to show themselves the equals of men: the women who travelled in omnibuses and horse-trams (the first tram was 'launched' in 1870), who sat on committees, demanded higher education and the vote, founded ladies' colleges and clubs, took part in sports.

A side issue of the social emancipation of women was the campaign for 'Rational Dress' in which Lady Harberton's divided skirts, known as 'dual garmenture', were much flaunted; and a side issue of 'Rational Dress' was the 'Woollen Movement', in which the unlovely garments advocated by Dr Gustave Jaeger played a conspicuous part – not outwardly conspicuous at first, since his original creations were named Sanitary Woollen Underwear. Wide publicity was achieved when Oscar Wilde took to lecturing on the subject and Bernard Shaw was seen walking in the West End in a complete suit made of Jaeger's knitted jersey fabric. The first Jaeger retail shop was opened in 1883 at Fore Street in the City.

Redfern was a tailor who, like John Morgan, began in Cowes and came to London on the crest of the tailored costume wave. He became very, very grand. The ground floor of his couture house resembled the Palm Court of a Grand Hotel, and ran right through from 26 Conduit Street to New Bond Street. Other great names of the period were Redmayne, Jay's, Reville & Rossiter, and Bradley's of Chepstow Place. Ladies who could not afford their prices were costumed to measure by the tailoring workrooms of department stores, and ordered their bespoke dresses from the Model Gown Departments. These were by no means inexpensive; and plenty of middle-class customers were beginning to find quite wearable fashions in the relatively new departments for ready-made clothes. The production of clothes made in factories, rather than in workrooms, was influential in the expansion of department stores. Other influences were cited by Lady Jeune in the *Fortnightly Review* of January 1896. She wrote of:

two very important changes which have contributed to the temptation of spending money nowadays. One is the gathering under one roof of all kinds of goods – clothing, millinery, groceries, furniture, in fact all the necessities of life. Nearly all the great shops in London are becoming vast stores. Many more people now come to London to shop and they prefer to make their purchases where they can concentrate their forces and diminish fatigue. The other is the large number of women now employed. Women are so much quicker than men, and they understand so much more readily what other women want. They can fathom the agony of despair as to the arrangement of colours, the alternative trimmings, the duration of a fashion, the depths of a woman's purse.

To finance their expansion, most of the leading stores became public companies during the 1880s and 1890s. This did not necessarily mean that they passed out of the hands of their founders' families, but some devoted customers feared their favourite shops would never be the same again. A columnist in a ladies' magazine wrote in 1898: 'There seems to be a small scare amongst certain members of my correspondents who imagine that their dearly beloved Marshall & Snelgrove's is going to be altered out of all recognition simply because it has been turned into a limited liability company.' No need for alarm. The shops were still very individual. Indeed, the 'nineties saw the zenith of the great individualists of retailing. Arthur Liberty, no longer a young man but still dedicated to the pursuit and purveyance of 'Art for Art's Sake'; John Lewis, a totally opposite character, tight-fisted despot underpaying his staff yet pouring out money in litigation against his ground landlord, Lord Howard de Walden, and carrying his individuality and obstinacy to the length of a term in Brixton for contempt of court; William Whiteley, Bayswater empire builder, always at war with the Paddington Council and making headlines in the local paper, running his own bus service to bring in customers from the northern suburbs; and Charles Digby Harrod, stubbornly resisting the installation of such modern gadgets as electric lighting and overhead cash carriers.

When Mr Harrod retired in 1891, Richard Burbidge became General Manager. Bursting with progressive ideas, he too had an oddly stubborn streak. His peculiar bugbear was that most desirable customer service, a lift. All the other stores were installing lifts, and his refusal might have lost much trade. In the outcome, however, it led to an invention that pioneered the moving staircase and gave Harrod's an unprecedented burst of publicity. This was simply a conveyor belt between two handrails. On the day of the inauguration in 1898, an attendant was stationed at the top to revive customers with sal volatile and/or cognac. But no one fainted. There was nothing but wide-eyed wonder. Even the reporter of the dignified *Pall Mall Gazette* was like a child at a pantomime, writing of 'an adaptation of the magic carpet of the fairy tale to the prosaic purposes of stairs'. The *Sketch* reporter wrote lyrically of being 'carried from floor to floor by a delightful movement which is both exhilarating and fascinating'. He, or she, was certainly carried away, since this magic carpet only went up one floor.

Meanwhile, a young retail adventurer was making news in another quarter. Walter Gamage, a Herefordshire farmer's son, had been apprenticed to a draper in the City and in 1878 set up shop for himself in Holborn. He was only twenty-one, a very tender age to start in business on one's own. But Gamage did not come of tender stock. He nailed a motto over his counter, *Tall oaks from little acorns grow*; and he tended his tiny shop from a five-foot frontage until it grew into a vast emporium, a conglomeration of Victorian buildings behind a grandiose neo-Gothic façade.

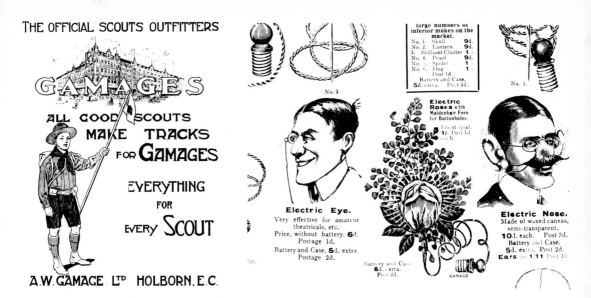

THE OFFICIAL SCOUTS OUTFITTERS

GAMAGES

ALL GOOD SCOUTS
MAKE TRACKS
FOR GAMAGES

EVERYTHING
FOR
EVERY SCOUT

A.W. GAMAGE LTD HOLBORN, E.C.

Electric Eye.
Very effective for amateur
theatricals, etc.
Price, without battery. **6**d.
Postage 1d.
Battery and Case, **5**d. extra.
Postage 2d.

Electric Roses with Maidenhair Fern for Buttonholes.
Finest qual.
1/- Post 1d each.

Electric Nose.
Made of waxed canvas,
semi-transparent.
10d. each. Post 2d.
Battery and Case.
5d. extra. Post 2d.
Ears ... **1/11** Post 2d.

large numbers of inferior makes on the market.
No. 1. Skull 9d.
No. 2. Lantern 9d.
3. Brilliant Cluster 1/-
No. 4. Pearl 9d.
No. 5. Spider 1/-
No. 6. Dog 1/-
Post 1d.
Battery and Case,
5d. extra. Post 2d.

As we have seen, Holborn had long ceased to be a fashionable shopping street. The success of Gamage's was not allied to the development of a new residential district, but to its convenience for City office workers in their lunch hour. It was masculine orientated, because there were still very few women in City offices. But many of the men who spent their lunch hours roaming around the bewildering interior of Gamage's – a maze of small rooms reached by narrow passages, up sudden flights of stairs – were family men living in suburban villas. The whole family could join father on a Saturday afternoon on a shopping spree at Gamage's. The children could be left happily in the toy department or the menagerie of live pets, mother could examine household linen and kitchen equipment, father could moon among garden mowers and carpentry tools. Gamage's was appointed outfitter for the scout movement and it was a great place for all kinds of campers. There was the Jaeger sleeping bag; the Gamage explorer's table and mosquito curtaining; the military hammock chair with glass holder for whisky; the collapsible rubber urinal for travelling. Gamage's was good, also, on games equipment. It did not have the cachet of Lillywhite's as sports supplier (after all Mr Gamage called his store 'The People's Popular Emporium'), but it supplied many sports associations and clubs. Sport was no longer only for the privileged at public schools, universities and country houses. Before the end of the century, nearly all big stores and most large business concerns had their staff sports clubs with grounds in the suburbs.

Gamage's great mail-order catalogue went to the middle-class and artisan homes of England, offering everything for the house, the garden, the nursery, the sportsman, for the man with a hobby, be it fretwork or taxidermy, for the do-it-yourself man, who was then called the home-handyman. There were even 'Asylum Requisites': lunatic locks, heavy warders' key chains, belts and fittings. Blessedly, there are always more children than lunatics, and toys were one of Walter Gamage's passions.

Gamage's Christmas Bazaar met all needs of the Christmas shopper before the First World War.

There were legendary tales of his travels in search of them: of being blinded by blizzards in the wilds of Michigan when tracking down the makers of an ingenious toy gun; of getting lost in an Austrian forest looking for the maker of a toy he had seen in a Vienna shop. He visited Frau Sieff's factory in the Black Forest, and became the largest British importer of her stuffed animals – Frau Sieff was the maker of the original teddy bear named after Teddy Roosevelt.

Gamage's sold its own make of bicycles for children and adults, and was in at the start of the combustion age with equipment for automobilists: fur-lined overboots, goggles, fur coats, stoves for the 'motor-house'. The Gamage 3 horsepower motor cycles, first sold in 1902, claimed to 'beat the flower of both English and foreign makes of often double the hp'. When he died, Walter Gamage was laid in state in the Motoring Department, with members of the staff mounting guard at the catafalque day and night. This may not have been in accordance with his own will; more likely it was an act of reverence by the son who succeeded him, since Walter Gamage had never been a showman in the sense of personal presentation, as was William Whiteley. Whiteley had a genius for free editorial publicity, and boasted that he never spent a penny on advertising. Fate abetted him by starting several spectacular fires in his store. In death he achieved maximum press coverage by being shot in his own office during the January sales by a man claiming to be his illegitimate son.

Most of the other big stores considered advertising essential. In 1894 Harrod's made advertising history by taking a full page in the *Daily Telegraph*, and two years later Swan & Edgar took space on the front page of the first issue of the *Daily Mail*. Fenwick of New Bond Street took a huge space in that most expensive of all advertising media to announce a sale of model gowns in 1903; but Gamage claimed to have been the first to make the *whole* of the *Dail Mail*'s front page – on 12 July 1904.

With all this, to some people's thinking, vulgar publicity, with the

162

DICKINS & JONES'
SUMMER SALE

Is now Proceeding.　As usual, their entire Stock is considerably Reduced in Price.　There is offered several Lots of Goods at less than Half their value.　Every endeavour will be made to execute all Post Orders promptly.　Illustrated Catalogue of Sale and Patterns Post Free on application.　They respectfully direct attention to the following details, and invite an early and frequent inspection of their Stock.

They have purchased for Cash, at less than one-third original price, from a Fabricant at Ste. Croix Grand Tonne, Pres Bayeux, Normandie, his large and exquisitely choice Stock of Needle-run black Chantilly Lace Scarfs, Half Shawls, Shawls, Lappets, Veils, &c., &c.　Detail as below :—

60 Scarfs, 2yds. 6in. long by 30in. wide, very suitable for Draping Dresses, or for Head-dress, or would be dressy and comfortable as a Neck Wrap for Seaside wear. Original price, 60s., for 19s. 6d. each.	15 Black Lace Shawls (would make a magnificent Lace Dress). Original price 300s., 250s. for 59s. 6d., 63s. each do. do.　　260s., 270s. ,, 65s. ,, 70s.
45 do. do. do.　50s.　 ,, 14s. 6d. each.	Original price.
7 do. do. do.　75s.　 ,, 25s. 0d. ,,	35 Black Lace Mantles　140s. for 70s.
16 do. do. do.　90s.　 ,, 29s. 6d. ,,	18 Black Lace Andalouse, 31s. 6d., for 11s. 6d. ,,
53 do. do. do.　100s. , 110s., ,, 35s. 6d., 38s. 6d.	27 do.　　　　21s., for 8s. 11d. ,,
19 do. do. do.　90s.　 ,, 31s. 6d. ,,	31 do.　　　　25s., for 10s. 9d. ,,
7 Half Shawls (may be employed for Draping Dresses).　　120s. for 39s. 6d.	83 Black Lace Coiffures, 3s. 6d. to 14s. 6d. ,,　　　　　　　　at 1s. 11d., 2s. 11d. ,,
7 do.　　　168s., 190s., ,, 53s., 59s. 6d.	182 Black Lace Veils, good shapes.
7 do.　　　147s., 120s., ,, 42s., 45s.	88 6d., for 1s. 11d. ,,
3 only do., Cream.　190s. ,, 59s. 6d.	244 do. do., very fine, 10s. 6d., for 2s. 11d. ,,
	370 do. do., best goods made. 16s. 6d., for 4s. 11d. ,,

REAL YAK FLOUNCINGS.

WITH NARROW LACES TO MATCH.

They are offering during the Sale a Manufacturer's Stock, value £3000, of this LOVELY REAL YAK, at less than one-third the original cost of production.　They will be found perfectly fresh and newly-made goods.

Costumes made of these Laces always look good, and very handsome, especially in Black, Cream, and Neutral Tints.

27in. BLACK, CREAM, and COLOURED REAL YAK FLOUNCINGS :

Usual prices, 10s. 6d., 11s. 6d., 14s. 6d., 15s. per yard.

Reduced to 3s. 3d., 3s. 11d., 4s. 6d., 4s. 11d. per yard.

36in. BLACK and COLOURED REAL YAK FLOUNCINGS :

Usual prices, 18s. 6d., 19s. 6d., 21s., 25s. 6d. per yard.

Reduced to 4s. 11d., 5s. 11d., 6s. 6d., 6s. 11d. per yard.

40in. BLACK, CREAM, and COLOURED REAL YAK LACE :

Usual prices, 21s., 25s. 6d., 31s. 6d., 36s. 6d. per yard.

Reduced to 6s. 6d., 6s. 11d., 7s. 11d., 8s. 11d. per yard.

This Illustration is Registered.

THE TENNIS OR BOATING JACKET,
in Fancy Striped Flannel and Plain Cream and Colours, well Shrunk and Tailor-made, reduced to 18s. 9d.; also in Plain and COVERT COATS, in Plain and Fancy Meltons, Drabs, and all Colours, with Fly Front, at 21s., same price to order.

Patterns and Forms for Self-measurement sent free.

THE "PRINCESS."

Lace Mantles (as Illustration) at half-price, and 100 others considerably reduced in price, commencing at 19s. 6d., 24s. 6d., 27s. 6d., 31s. 6d., 38s. 6d., 42s., to 70s.　Also

175 Mantillas of rich Silk Lace, full size, can be worn illustrated, at the following prices, 14/6, 17/9, 21/-, 2/6, 29/6, 33/6, 39/6, 42/-, 55/-.

Special Makes in Rich Blonde, Grenade, &c., most charming Mantillas, at 75/-, 84/-, 93/-, 100/-, 115/-, 5s. 19s., £7. 7s. Any of these goods can be sent on probation.

Lace Boas.—The New Lace Boa can be had in Black Silk Chantilly Lace, and Mechlin Lace in Cream or Beige, 1½ yards long, reduced to 7s. 6d. to 12s. 3d.; 2 yards long, 11s. 6d. to 16s. 9d.; 2½ and 2½ yards long, 18s. 6d. to 29s.; any length made to order.

2CO Evening Wraps, of Silk Chenille, with fringe all round, in Black, White, Cream, Sky, Pink, Cardinal, Grenat, Myrtle, Peacock, Tabac, Old Gold, Orange, &c., at 15s. 6d. A great luxury.

300 other very Charming Designs, at 25s.

300 Algerian Wraps, in Black and Gold Stripes, Red and Gold, Blue and Gold, Bronze and Gold, Cream and Gold, nearly 2 yards square, at 4s. 11d. each; chiefly in Cream, at 7s. 11d. each.

Mantles.—The Stock of Mantles, summer Capes, and Mantles suitable for early autumn wear, will be cleared at greatly reduced prices.

500 Mantles.—A small Stock purchased at 50 per cent. will be included in the sale, at half price, including elegant Jet Mantles, Summer Capes, and long Ladies' Jackets, &c., from 16s. 9d. to 63s.

Ladies' Underclothing. — The Stock, consisting only of high-class Goods made by hand on the Premises, by Nuns in Convents, and by Scotch and Irish peasant women, as at all former sales, will be cleared at great reduction in price. Ladies contemplating

matrimony will find this a favourable opportunity for obtaining superior articles at the price of ordinary goods.

SAMPLES FREE.

Tea and Dressing Gowns greatly reduced in price.

Gloves.—The entire Stock at reduced prices. Qualities guaranteed.　There are Twenty Lots set aside for clearing out at a great reduction, detailed catalogues of which can be had free.

Hose.—200 dozen Ladies' Black pure spun Silk Stockings, at 2s. 6d. and 3s. 11d. per pair.

Lace Dresses.—Lovely Lace Robes, in Cream and Beige, from 19s. 9d. to 30s., for 5 yards of wide and 5 narrow, sufficient to make light, cool, and pretty dress.

Rich Silk Black Chantilly Flounce, 36 inches, 4s. 11d.; 42 inches, 6s. 3d. per yard ; Rich Black Silk Chantilly, 40 inches wide, very rich quality, reduced to 6s. 3d. per yard ; Black Spanish Lace Flouncing, 40 inches wide, reduced to 3s. 6d. per yard.

Black Chantilly Lace, for Mantles and Dress Trimming.　Several lovely designs will be found in the Sale, some at half their value, all greatly reduced in price.　A complete set of patterns sent free on application.

Beaded Tabliers, Beaded Panels, Beaded Laces, at a great reduction in price, in Black and Pearl, in all qualities, and in great variety. Panels, from 3s. 6d.; Tabliers, from 6s. 3d.; Beaded Nets, from 1s. 4½d. to 29s., 27 inches wide ; Beaded Gaze, for Mantles, in lovely designs, 27 inches wide, from 6s. 11d. per yard.

Antique Valenciennes Lace.—A design greatly appreciated, in Cream and Beige, at the following reduced prices, 3½d., 4d., 6d., 7½d., 10½d. per yard.

REAL TORCHON LACE.

Our Stock always contains the largest possible assortment of these goods ; every choice pattern, all bought direct from the workers.　This Lace is the most durable trimming for ladies' and children's underclothing.　During the Sale the prices will be found considerably reduced, commencing at 1s. to 25s. for 12 yards.　The largest collection of patterns ever seen can be had free on application.

POINT DE PARIS.

A new Thread Lace, specially adapted for trimming underwear, very strong and effective.　Reduced prices from 3½d., 4½d., 5d., 6½d., 8½d., to 1s. per yard.

NURSERY EMBROIDERY.

A most durable article for trimming Children's underwear.　Outwears any material it might be

attached to.　Can be had at Reduced Prices during the Sale, in three different designs, 1s. 3d., 1s. 9d., 2s., 2s. 6d., 2s. 11d., 3s. 9d., 4s. 3d.　Also in Ecru colour, 2s. 11d., 4s. 3d., 5s. 6d.　Send for Patterns, free.

White Cambric Embroidery, for Ladies' Underclothing.　We are now in a position to supply goods direct from the loom, having made arrangements to employ a number of machines continually making for us, thus saving the intermediate profits.　We shall sell Embroidery in our Sale at 2½d., 3d., 4d., 5d., 6d., to 2s. 6d. per yard ; usually sold at one-third more.　We shall have a splendid assortment to offer. Patterns Free.　Also in Ecru.

COSTUMES.

All the Paris Model Costumes will be cleared at Half Price.　Washing Costumes, Fête Costumes, Dinner Costumes in great variety at tempting prices.

TENNIS.

A very large assortment of the New Unshrinkable Lawn Tennis Flannels, from 10½d. to 2s. per yard.

Patterns sent on application.

CURTAINS.

The Stock of Lace Curtains is very large and choice. They will be all greatly reduced in price to effect a clearance, and will be found well worthy of inspection.

The Sale is now proceeding, and will Continue during JULY.

HANOVER HOUSE, 232, 234, REGENT ST., LONDON, W.

turning of family businesses into public companies, and the start of big firms taking over small firms, the fashion historian Georgiana Hill, writing in 1893, foresaw

the grinding of the individual trader between the wheels of the monoliths. The old methods are worn out, the fierceness of competition has developed an elaborate and expensive system of advertising on which manufacturers and merchants are, practically, dependent for success. Consequently, few can stand alone. A business, as soon as it becomes large, passes from the hands of the individual to those of a syndicate or company. It is an age of big combinations, and those who either cannot or will not fall in with the new order of things are frequently left behind and crushed.

Miss Hill, in her role of Cassandra, might have included among the menaces to individuality the growth of manufacturers' multiple chains. The first was that of the Singer Sewing Machine Company, which opened a shop in Glasgow in 1856 and by 1877 had over 160 Singer shops throughout Britain. Fleming Reid, spinners, opened their first Scotch Wool & Hosiery shop in Greenock in 1881, and by 1910 had over two hundred. The cheap shoe chains, such as those of George Oliver and of Freeman, Hardy & Willis, multiplied exceedingly from the 1870s. In groceries, John Sainsbury, who opened his first shop in Drury Lane in 1869, was ahead of Thomas Lipton; but Lipton put on a tremendous spurt and finished the century with 245 shops. In pharmacies, Jesse Boot of Nottingham had by then gained a foothold in London by buying the 65 shops of Day's Drug Stores; and the first step into the London area of Marks & Spencer's Penny Bazaars was at Brixton in 1903.

Nevertheless, looking back to the 1890s from the present day, it does seem that the gracious days of shopping were by no means over. Call it service or call it servility, the customer was still treated with a deference, even a reverence, which was rarely her due. At Gorringe's, in Buckingham Palace Road, it was the rule that no assistant must ever say 'Good morning, Madam' unless first addressed by a customer. At Liberty's it was forbidden, when a customer requested his or her purchase to be delivered, to ask the name and address – assistants were expected to know all their account customers by sight. An employee of Dickins & Jones who joined the firm around the turn of the century recorded in some notes: 'The trade in those days was steady and [there was] plenty to do. All the elite arriving in carriage and pairs, cabs, etc. were attended by commissionaires and page boys on every door in their white gloves. Flowers in season could always be seen over all the windows.'

The 'serving through' system obtained in all high-class stores: the impressive gentleman in morning coat inside the main shop door who summoned a shopwalker to escort you to the counter you required and place a chair for you, and the pantomime in reverse to see you out of the shop and into your carriage. At Liberty's the shopwalkers were called cicerones, and there were also lady cicerones who wore floor length velvet gowns with trains all through the short-skirted twenties, right up to 1932. At some shops, including Swan & Edgar, the unfortunate assistant whose customer decided against purchasing was not allowed on pain of dismissal to let her go without first summoning a shopwalker. All large stores had extensive workrooms, where skilled dressmakers made clothes to measure and altered ready-made garments to fit. Mourning orders were completed with especial urgency. Since etiquette decreed that widows and daughters must not be seen out of doors before the funeral, shops 'waited upon' the house of mourning. At 'Black Peter Robinson' a brougham was kept ready harnessed to set off at a summons without a moment's delay. A retired member of the firm has described this macabre spectacle: 'The coachmen were in black from head to foot, with crape hat bands and arm bands, and whips with crape bows. Two lady fitters, also clad completely in black, sat in the brougham, equipped with patterns and designs'. As the brougham raced through the streets, it must have been as thrilling a sight to watch as a fire engine. The finished mourning garments were, of course, delivered in time for the funeral.

When Victoria died, the whole nation was plunged into mourning. For the drapery trade it was an unprecedented challenge, recalled in some notes written by Mr J. B. Smith, who joined Dickins & Jones a year or so before. They had been busy filling every window with household linen, which in those days was all white: 'The day Queen Victoria died we were on the eve of the White Sales. By the next morning everything was turned to black – it was one of the biggest transformations in the history of the trade. Everything that could be dyed was used to meet the colossal demand.'

George du Maurier's acute comment on one of the pressures suffered by shop assistants.

ALL THE DIFFERENCE!

Haberdasher (to Assistant who has had the "swoop"). "WHY HAS THAT LADY GONE WITHOUT BUYING?"
Assistant. "WE HAVEN'T GOT WHAT SHE WANTS."
Haberdasher. "I'LL SOON LET YOU KNOW, MISS, THAT I KEEP YOU TO SELL WHAT I'VE GOT, AND NOT WHAT PEOPLE WANT!"

15 Edwardian high noon

A John Barnes van, c. 1908.

Opposite:
Selfridge's offering of a 'New and Wonderful Shopping Centre' to the London of 1909.

THE VILLAGE of Hampstead developed more as a little country town than as a suburb. Pleasing terraces of modest houses with gardens at the rear were built for professional, literary and scholarly people. In the steep, narrow High Street were all the shops necessary for day-to-day purchases. They were small, old-fashioned, friendly shops – no popular emporium polluted Hampstead's quiet country-town atmosphere. Indeed, there was no department store nearer than Oxford Street until 1900, when the John Barnes store was built in Finchley Road – a strategic position, since its customer catchment area included not only Hampstead and the less elite Golders Green, but also sequestered St John's Wood. In the last-named leafy little suburb, detached and semi-detached villas had been built within their own walled gardens. It was the quintessence of *rus in urbe*; and its pretty, embowered houses gained the romantic reputation of being love-nests for expensive mistresses. This does not seem to have deterred people of unquestionable respectability from making their homes in St John's Wood. Trollope allowed Lady Amelia de Courcy to live there; and her sister, Lady Alexandrina, would like to have moved to St John's Wood also, but her husband, very sensitive of the social status of a London address, refused to live north of the New Road – that is, Marylebone Road, as it later became. Even to live north of Oxford Street was socially 'impossible' in the eyes of some people.

The John Barnes store was financed by a consortium of six retailers, which included Edwin Jones, one of the rescuers of the Brixton Bon Marché. John Barnes himself was a director of John Barker's in Kensington: but less than a year after the new company was floated, he was drowned when the steamship *Stella* ran aground in fog off Guernsey. Thus he never saw the store which still carries his name. After the shipwreck, Edwin Jones was made chairman and the building was completed – an ultra-modern store with fifty departments under one roof all carpeted in best Axminster, a central passenger lift, and Lamson Pneumatic Tubing to save delays at cash desks. At that time, only three other London shops had the latter system: the Bon Marché, Robinson & Cleaver, the Belfast linen-drapers who opened a branch in Regent Street in 1894, and Roberts of Stratford. The John Barnes building had

SELFRIDGE'S London's New & Wonderful
Shopping Centre
Dedicated to Woman's Service - devoted to the Children's
Needs - the Man's Best Buying Place - with best assorted
Stocks at London's Lowest Prices:
NOW OPEN TO THE WORLD   OXFORD STREET
LONDON.W.

F.V.Poole
'09

"London receiving her
Newest Institution"

accommodation for 400 assistants, with three dining-rooms, one for the buyers and one for each sex of the rank and file – the curious custom of segregating the sexes at meals was a long time dying. *The Draper's Record* rather grudgingly commented that, given a good locality, there was 'no reason why a big trading establishment should not be a mammoth establishment from the start, without undergoing the laborious and time-wasting process of the gradual addition of department on department', which, it added, 'was the British method and had the crowning merit of safety'. Perhaps these doubts were justified, since it was over ten years before John Barnes began to make substantial profits; by which time Gordon Selfridge had arrived on the British shopping scene and had proved beyond all possible shadow of doubt that 'a mammoth establishment from the start' *could*, by new methods, be profitable beyond the dreams of cautious British retailers.

Gordon Selfridge first visited London in the 1890s while still an employee of Marshall Field's of Chicago. His biographer, Reginald Pound, described his impressions on this visit: 'He was amused by the ridiculous deference of the shopwalkers. . . . "The stores and larger shops tried to reproduce the subdued and disciplined atmosphere of the gentleman's mansion". He pooh-poohed the snobbery of thinking "it was better to do an exclusive trade than a big trade".' The grandiose neo-Classical building that Selfridge conjured up in Oxford Street in 1909 was to show the British what retailing was all about. Public curiosity had been whetted by frequent stories in the press during the year it was being built; and as the opening drew near an immense advertising campaign was launched. Selfridge had summoned from Chicago Marshall Field's head window-dresser to prepare dramatic displays in the windows, which were kept lighted until midnight. It was entirely new for an English store to have a display man on the staff – department buyers themselves dressed the windows allocated to their departments. On the opening day, the public was invited to walk round all the departments and the 'aerial garden', use the writing, reading and rest rooms, the post office and information bureau, without the slightest obligation to buy anything. Selfridge declared he intended his store to be a social centre, not a shop; later his advertisements asked, 'WHY NOT SPEND THE DAY AT SELFRIDGE'S?'

It was women, of course, who had days to spend; and Selfridge orientated his store to the desires and devices of the feminine heart, placing the perfumery counters just inside the main entrance, so that passers on the pavement were seduced inside by the enticing scents. Not even Selfridge, the social climber from the New World with no knowledge of London society, can have expected that the upper classes would spend a day at Selfridge's. He was aiming at middle-class women, newly emancipated, with much more say than they had ever had before in the disbursement of the family income. On the ground floor, the American ice-cream soda fountain was a treat for the children when on holiday; and the garden on the roof was yet another novel attraction. In 1912 he introduced the Bargain Basement, which attracted husbands as well. Selfridge's was not only the talk of the town, but of the country.

For visitors to London, whether from the provinces or from abroad, it became as essential to visit Selfridge's as to see Westminster Abbey and the Tower. Other Oxford Street retailers benefited from the fame Selfridge brought to the street. Even the old established drapery business of Thomas Lloyd, occupying the next eight shops to Selfridge, at first received a worthwhile spin-off; but in 1914, when Selfridge acquired more property in Orchard Street and Somerset Street, Lloyd's was also engulfed.

At the other end of Oxford Street Mr Bourne and his brother-in-law Mr Hollingsworth were prospering. They had started with a small drapery shop in Westbourne Grove in 1894, but the domination in that district of William Whiteley and William Owen left them no potential for expansion. Moving to 116 and 118 Oxford Street in 1902, they enjoyed rapid expansion. Indeed, they acquired a complete island site, goal of all ambitious shopkeepers, before Selfridge achieved his. Mr Hollingsworth once made a list of all the tenants who had to be shifted before he got full possession of his island site. The list is given exactly as he wrote it:

1 pub	A brothel
1 dairy	1 private residence
A branch of Finch's	A wholesale lace merchant
A barber	A nest of Polish tailors
A coffee house	A sweet shop
A carpet layer	Doan's Backache Pills

A costume manufacturer	A cigarette factory (Savory's)
A wholesale milliner	A wholesale blouse maker (Frances)
A retail milliner	A wine-merchant's cellar
A music publisher	A soda water manufacturer
A musical instrument shop (German)	A jeweller
	A baby linen manufacturer
A palmist	A wallpaper merchant
A beauty parlour	An estate agent
British headquarters, New Columbia Gramophone Co.	2 solicitors
	1 chapel

Neither Bourne & Hollingsworth nor Selfridge attracted the carriage trade, as did the older Oxford Street stores. A retired employee of Peter Robinson nostalgically recalled in conversation: 'Oxford Street was a superior shopping street until Bourne & Hollingsworth brought the general trade and then Selfridge's. We were family drapers . . . the carriages would drive up and the duchesses would step out. Customers would discuss Sunday's sermon with you, give all their family news, and say their married daughter would be in during the afternoon.' Of course, 'the general trade' was probably what Bourne & Hollingsworth aimed at, since they went to 'the wrong end of Oxford Street', the east end. But at least they were on the right side of the street, the sunny side. Shops on the south side of Oxford Street, where the pavements are in shadow until late evening, have never been as successful as those on the north.

Aloof from the general trade in Oxford Street, Debenham & Freebody, the *grande dame* of Wigmore Street, was at her zenith in the Edwardian period. She had stood her ground, gradually increasing it, longer than any other of the shops that had grown into department stores – Fortnum & Mason, although established much earlier, was still only a grocery shop in this period. Debenham's was the earliest retail empire builder. Before 1830 it had acquired a shop in the fashionable spa of Cheltenham, and later started a branch in Harrogate. Before the end of the century it was buying up London firms of high repute: Nicholay of Oxford Street, furriers by appointment to Queen Victoria and the reigning families of Russia, Austria, Prussia, Belgium and Spain; the linen house of Capper's, suppliers to Buckingham Palace; the Maison Helbronner of New Bond Street, established in 1834 as Ecclesiastical, Heraldic and Domestic Embroiderers; and in 1900, most notable acquisition of all, Howell & James, whose stock included rare tapestries, brocades and embroideries, antique silver, jewellery and glass, pewter and ceramics.

All the time Debenham's was also extending the wholesale drapery side of its business, to New York, Canada, South Africa, Australia. In 1907 it crowned its glory with a new building on the old site, architecturally a much more restrained and dignified building than the other emporiums built in that period of grandiose stores – as, for instance, Harrod's enormity in Doulton terracotta. A Franco-British Exhibition was held in London in 1908, and Debenham's issued a souvenir booklet for visitors: 'You may, if you wish, have lunch or tea at very moderate charges in the quiet, elegant Restaurant, to which a

Bourne & Hollingsworth and its millinery department in the first decade of the twentieth century.

Harrod's terracotta exterior – by 1911 the building covered four and a half acres; and (opposite) a mantle showroom, c. 1913, typical of the spacious grandeurs within.

Smoking-room and Gentlemen's Cloakroom are attached. The Ladies' Club Room is open to lady visitors, who may there read the papers and magazines, telephone, write letters or meet their friends, and adjoining it is a luxuriously appointed suite of Dressing and Retiring Rooms.' Provincial ladies could change for an evening engagement in this Ritz of retiring rooms, its spacious private cubicles each having, in addition to the essential sanitary fitment, a dressing-table, chair, long-mirror and marble wash-hand basin.

Dickins & Jones also did some empire building from the 1890s onward, when they acquired Lewis & Allenby, most famous of all silk mercers, Allison's of Regent Street, and the baby-linen house of Balls & Flint. They next swooped upon Redmayne, celebrated couturier of Bond Street, and then bought up the stock of Hilditch's, silk mercers in the City, and acquired George Hitchcock's of St Paul's Churchyard. The founders' families were still in control: two Dickins, father and son, on the board, and Sir John Pritchard Jones managing director – until 1914. In that year, Harrod's made its first takeover, the victim being Dickins & Jones.

Harrod's celebrated its Diamond Jubilee in 1909, when it was claimed to be 'the shrine of fashion' and 'a recognized social rendezvous; in fact, one of the few smart rendezvous acknowledged and patronized by Society. At the appointment bureau, notes can be left for friends.' There was also a bureau for theatre tickets, a tourist office, post office, circulating library, and music room. Harrod's claimed to have been pioneers of shopping by telephone, with an all-night service; and also to have been first to organize special shopping trains from the country, and first with free delivery to country customers. The validity of this last claim is doubtful, since Whiteley's offered a free delivery service to Brighton in 1886. From Harrod's Diamond Jubilee booklet we learn that the Gentlemen's Club was 'furnished in the style of the Georgian period carried out in richly carved and moulded mahogany', while the Ladies Club was furnished in a more feminine Adam style featuring figured satinwood, 'the chairs upholstered in green corded silk, tastefully decorated with appliqué embroidery. The Retiring Room, fitted out in marble, has windows of stained cathedral glass, and walls covered with panelled Brecchi Sanguine, Pavannazzi, Levantine marble, and onyx panels, the whole rendering an unique effect.' Unique indeed.

Harrod's customers belonged to the pedigree dog-owning classes: 'Dogs of all breeds may be seen chained at the entrance at all hours of the day, awaiting the return of their owners from within.' It was William Whiteley who took the first brave step of forbidding man's best friend to enter his premises. An immediate decline in trade had been expected to follow this unsporting, not to say un-British, veto: but, as it turned out, Whiteley's suffered no noticeable withdrawal of two-legged customers, and the Army & Navy Stores soon took the controversial bit between its teeth and insisted upon dogs being left outside.

Harrod's Diamond Jubilee year was the very year of Selfridge's opening; and Harrod's chose the actual week of Selfridge's highly dramatized inauguration to put on a series of decorous concerts, with Landon Ronald conducting the London Symphony Orchestra. Selfridge must surely have been speaking sarcastically when he said Harrod's had 'put up a magnificent counterblast to our opening'. His own blast was given by an army trumpeter blowing a fanfare from the first-floor parapet above the main entrance as the Selfridge flag was unfurled. Harrod's did, however, have some more popular publicity than the symphony concerts. In the musical comedy *Our Miss Gibbs* at the Gaiety Theatre some of the scenes were set at 'Garrod's', and fifty of the costumes were designed and made in Harrod's workrooms.

Grand and gracious as the Edwardian stores were, the *crème de la crème* scorned to shop at them. The Edwardian period was the *belle époque* of those mature beauties whom the hatter Frederick Willis has described so perfectly in his *A Book of London Yesterdays*. 'Oh, those Edwardian women! to see them in their glory one had to be in Old Bond Street between the hours of four and six in the afternoon. The street was full of their carriages, and there was an air of reverence in the shops as they entered.' These goddesses shopped in Bond Street, not at 'Garrod's'. And Frederick Willis asserts that:

No man of discrimination would dream of buying his hat at a big store. The really smart hatters were accommodated in small, old-fashioned shops, and a strange intimacy existed between customer and hatter. . . . When a son came of age his father brought him in to be introduced. These striplings of the aristocracy were, of course warmly welcomed. What caused alarm in the hatter's heart was when a customer brought his wife with him. . . . When I saw them alighting from their French victorias, all frills, fascination, and French perfume, my heart sank. Doors were opened for them, chairs were placed for them, and they sat down with a gracious smile and prepared to exercise their talent for throwing a spanner into the works.

The Edwardian period was the great period of the topper. Mr Willis again: 'We could tell the social standing of a customer by the way he asked for it. If he described it as a silk hat we knew he belonged to suburbia and respectability, if he asked for a top hat he belonged to the City (Stock Exchange or Mincing Lane), but if he demanded a topper he was out of the top drawer.' Top drawer gentlemen called at their hatters every day to have their toppers ironed while they waited; and all round the walls of Mr Willis's shop were white boxes on which were stencilled the names of 'people so important that they could not wait for

their hats to be ironed but had to have one always ready for them when they dashed in'.

The wives and daughters of these distinguished gentlemen did not patronize department stores. They had their own milliners for hats, their exclusive dressmakers or couturiers for gowns, their tailoring houses for costumes. The great couture houses of the Edwardian period were Reville & Rossiter, Russell & Allen, Redfern, Mascotte of 89 Park Street (directed by Mrs Cyril Drummond, herself 'in Society'), Fred Bosworth, famed for his sporting clothes and walking costumes, the London branch of Worth in Grosvenor Street, Bradley's of Chepstow Place, and Lucile of Hanover Square. Lucile, who in private life was Lady Duff Gordon, sister of Elinor Glyn, the writer of deliciously risqué Society novels, was also very daring. She introduced *crêpe de chine* underwear, and was the first couture house to have mannequin parades in which the model girls did not have their flesh completely covered with black satin *maillots*.

In her reminiscences, she described her horror at seeing in a Paris couture house 'lovely evening dresses in pale shades being worn by girls whose arms and necks, in dingy black satin, emerged from the low-cut decolletés . . . as a guarantee of the respectability of the establishment,

Edwardiana: the Bond Street scene in 1902; and disdain on both sides as models parade before a customer the year before.

175

*From the Fenwick's catalogue,
1907.*

only very plain girls were employed.' Lucile engaged six beautiful girls with the fine figures admired by Edwardians. None of them weighed much under eleven stone, and some were six-footers. She took them to New York, Chicago and Paris, and they all married millionaires. Modern millionaires tend to be small men, so it may be fortunate that the ideal of feminine beauty is less monumental now than in Edwardian times. Mr Hiley, fashion dictator at Jay's in the 1890s when it blossomed out from being solely a mourning house, is sometimes credited with having been the first to employ live mannequins in London; in fact they wore black combinations similar to the *maillots* worn in Paris couture houses. After Lucile's lovelies had broken down inhibitions, the more progressive stores realized what an attraction mannequin parades would be to their customers. In 1909, Harrod's announced that 'the Costume Department displays gowns on living models, some of the smartest figures in London being especially employed for this purpose'.

Readymade clothes were by now an important section of department-store business; but the only clothes sold readymade in Bond Street were expensive blouses and handmade underwear – handmade because *ladies* never wore machine-stitched underclothes. When Mr Fenwick of Newcastle opened a branch of his very exclusive dressmaking establishment in New Bond Street in 1891, he too held aloof from ready-to-wear. For a provincial retailer to come to Bond Street at all was an act of daring equivalent to a London shop opening a branch in the Faubourg St Honoré. It would have been unthinkable for him to have come to *Old* Bond Street, as is made clear by Frederick Willis:

Between Old and New Bond Streets was an impregnable social barrier that nobody ever attempted to cross. Up to 1914, Old Bond Street was the quintessence of aristocratic shopping. . . . Shopkeepers in Old Bond Street were not tradesmen but critics, connoisseurs, and authorities on the goods they dealt in. . . . After the first war, the LCC became active in tidying up the names of London Streets. It was then proposed to combine Old and New Bond Streets and call the result Bond Street. New Bond Street residents were quite agreeable to the change, but the howls of execration that came from Old Bond Street shook even the LCC into an understanding of the enormous gaffe they had made.

Bond Street, both Old and New, escaped the organized attack upon West End shop windows launched by suffragettes on 1 March 1912. At 4 o'clock in the afternoon, almost every window from Piccadilly Circus up Regent Street and along much of Oxford Street was broken by women with hammers they had hidden in their muffs or some other part of their dress. The headlines in next morning's papers were predictable, and readers' letters in the following days expressed the nation's outrage. Mrs Watson, a member of a county education authority, wrote to the *Standard*: 'I can hardly imagine any lady, of whatever political party she may be, who does not feel the utmost disgust on reading in Saturday's paper of the public degradation of womanhood. Words fail me, and I am oddly reminded of the time-honoured saying in *Punch*: "It's worse than wicked; it's vulgar".' More than two hundred women were arrested – for damage to property, not vulgarity. They were mostly students,

Mahogany, Oak, or Walnut.
39/6

Harrod's hall stand: just under £2 for the 1895 customer. And one of its provision counters in the same period.

nurses and artists, though those sent to prison included the distinguished musician Dr (later Dame) Ethel Smythe.

That sensational happening apart, the West End shops retained their
serene dignity until the fateful August of 1914. As the retail magnates
waxed richer, they gathered knighthoods, even baronetcies, and some
became squires of country estates. But the shopocracy – *Punch*'s term –
failed to achieve social equality with the blood aristocracy. Sir Thomas
Lipton, the 'Boating Grocer', poured out money on yachts to challenge
America in the America's Cup, but was not elected to the Royal Yacht
Squadron until the very end of his life. As for shop assistants, their lot
was still lamentable. The Shops Act of 1911 came into force on 1 May
1912, making a half-day closing mandatory; but salaries were still very
low, and the living-in system continued with all its indignities and
restrictions. Staff rules at one shop included the following: 'Men
employees are given one evening each week for courting purposes, and
two if they go to prayer-meeting regularly.'

In contrast, the founders of some famous stores, or their descendants,
ran their firms in a paternal way, and this paternalism was repaid by great
staff loyalty. For one thing the Edwardian period, like the Victorian, was
one in which the boss worked as hard, and was *seen* to work as hard, as
his employees. Sir Richard Burbidge always began his working day at
Harrod's at 7 a.m., and had his breakfast with the supervisors. Such
stores also retained the loyalty of their customers, generation after
generation, daughters inheriting from mothers an affection for the

family's favourite shop. Osbert Lancaster, in *All Done from Memory*, writes:

It is difficult nowadays to realise how very personal was then the relationship, even in London, between shop-keeper and customer and the enormous importance, comparable almost to that attained by rival churches, which late Victorian and Edwardian ladies attached to certain stores. All my female relatives had their own favourites, where some of them had been honoured customers for more than half a century, and their arrival was greeted by frenzied bowing on the part of the frock-coated shopwalkers, and where certain of the older assistants stood to them almost in the relationship of confessors, receiving endless confidences on the state of their health, the behaviour of their pets and the general iniquity of the Liberal Government.

The golden high-noon of the British Empire was reflected in the prosperity of London's specialist furnishing firms. Hampton's, Maple's, Waring & Gillow, Liberty were all kept at full stretch with decorating contracts for the great luxury hotels that were being built, the gentlemen's clubs, company boardrooms, City banks, insurance offices, department stores, and the massive blocks of 'mansion flats' going up in Kensington, for whose furnishing the word 'mansion' describes the style. Period furniture was what their patrons demanded, with plenty of panelling on the walls, elaborate plasterwork ceilings and thick carpets. There were also commissions for the magnificent ocean liners of the day, which were furnished as floating hotels with Tudor dining saloons, Adam libraries, cabins decorated in the chintzy manner of country-house bedrooms, and palm courts as in so many non-floating hotels. Splendid private yachts were furnished regardless of nautical relevance; and Waring's advised Kaiser Wilhelm on the décor of his royal yacht. Thomas Goode of South Audley Street numbered maharajas and Eastern potentates, the Empress of Russia and other European royalty, among its customers for costly ceramics and glass from England's famous potteries and glassworks. Foreign royalty came frequently to London to choose furniture and furnishings. The Crown Princess of Greece wrote a rapturous letter to her mother, quoted by James Pope-Hennessy in his *Queen Mary*: 'We spent I don't know how many hours at Maple and Liberty! I *screamed* at the things to Tino's horror, but they were too lovely! – Divine shops!!'

Liberty's executed decorating and cabinet-making contracts in far away continents for Indian princes and South African tycoons. In Europe its design team worked in Rotterdam, Alsace, Venice, Monaco, Genoa, Budapest; and it was said that the firm was commissioned for work of one kind or another by nearly all the *haute noblesse* of France. In the summer of 1914 a member of the Liberty staff was learning Russian before going to St Petersburg to supervise work for the Czar; and a contract was actually in progress for the Archduke Franz Ferdinand of Austria when he was assassinated – the assassination that lit the fuse to the First World War.

PEACE

'The Peace of the Great Release' HENLEY'S 'RHYMES & RHYTHMS'

DERRY & TOMS

Business had not been as usual during the Great War, despite the slogans at the beginning. Would anything be the same again?

After 1918, the London shopping scene was little changed, although the glitter had gone out. There was less conspicuous costliness, but still a carriage trade, now chauffeur driven. William Weaver, one of twelve doormen at Harrod's, remembers how he called up customers' cars: 'The car drives up with chauffeur and footman. I open the car door, the footman puts the rug over Madam or Sir. One day I called the wrong car, and the chauffeur had driven to Victoria before he realised he'd got the wrong lady.' The retail magnates were also chauffeur driven. John Lewis descended from his Hampstead residence to Oxford Street in a resplendent Rolls Royce. Total despot in his shop until death removed him at the age of ninety-two, he was a confirmed agnostic. 'John Lewis's faith', said his son Spedan, 'was in the divine right of employers.' He was fanatically hostile to trade unions. In 1920 four-fifths of his staff of five hundred struck for more pay, for permission to leave the shop during meal breaks, and for more democracy in living-in arrangements. 'If I see them on their hands and knees I shall not take them back', John Lewis declared. It was a time of high unemployment and the strikers' jobs were easily filled.

In post-war Mayfair – the Mayfair of Michael Arlen and the Bright Young People – a new species of shopkeeper opened chic little 'Madam shops' selling clothes that were 'quite too utterly divine'. There were also titled ladies who played at hat shops without loss of social status, and gentlemen of the New Poor who adventured upon antique shops.

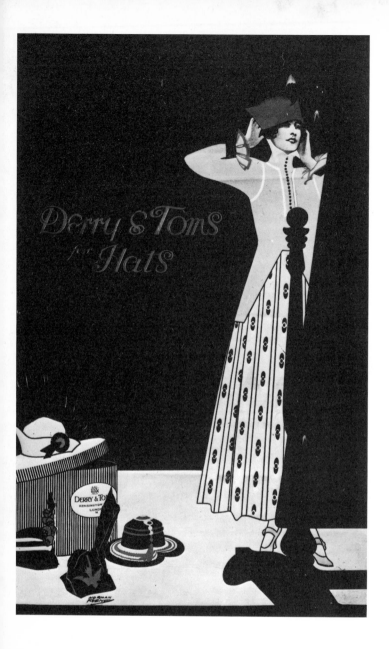

Between the wars: shopping at Woolland's in 1922; Derry & Toms incapsulates the style of the early 'thirties.

But the Old Bond Street shops retained their aloof dignity, and there was still a faithful clientele for Mayfair's exclusive dressmaking establishments. In Regent Street, Oxford Street, Knightsbridge and Kensington, department stores continued the serving-through system, with frock-coated shopwalkers conducting customers to chairs at the counters they desired. Staff hierarchy was immutable, and an assistant at Marshall & Snelgrove in those days remembers that 'the model gown buyers behaved like queens'. There were still apprentices. Clara Lloyd, who was apprenticed to Liberty's embroidery workrooms from 1918 to 1924, recalls with pride how they worked through a ten-hour day with a three-

quarter-hour break for lunch. 'We apprentices were respectful to our elders, and too much talking was discouraged. We listened to everything. Our instruction, of course, was of the first importance.'

In the smaller drapers and in all the domestic trades, customer service and retailing methods continued as in Edwardian times throughout the period between the wars. Grocers and butchers still 'waited upon' families for orders, and the baker delivered daily. It was from 1945 onwards that great changes came. The social revolution was inevitably accompanied by a shopping revolution – a revolution that awaits another historian.

Bibliographical guide to sources

When a book is edited with considerable introduction and notes, it is listed here under the name of the editor as well as that of the author.

W. H. ABLETT *Reminiscences of an Old Draper*, from articles written for the *Warehouseman and Drapers' Trade Journal* during 1872, Sampson Low, Marston, Searl & Rivington, 1876

RUDOLF ACKERMANN *Microcosm of London*, Ackermann, 1808–9

ALISON ADBURGHAM *Shops and Shopping, 1800–1914*, Allen & Unwin, 1964

ALISON ADBURGHAM *Liberty's – A Biography of a Shop*, Allen & Unwin, 1975

DAVID ALEXANDER *Retailing in England during the Industrial Revolution*, University of London, the Athlone Press, 1970

HENRY ANGELO *Reminiscences*, Henry Colburn, 1828

JOHN ASHTON *Social Life in the Reign of Queen Anne*, Chatto & Windus, 1883

JANE AUSTEN *Letters to her Sister Cassandra and Others*, ed. R. W. Chapman, Oxford University Press, 1952

JANE AUSTEN *Pride and Prejudice*, 1813

T. C. BARKER and MICHAEL ROBBINS, *A History of London Transport, Vol. I, 19th Century*, Allen & Unwin, 1963

ALFRED R. BENNETT *London and Londoners in the 1850s and 1860s*, Fisher Unwin, 1924

JAMES BOSWELL *London Journal, 1762–3*, ed. Frederick A. Pottle, Heinemann, 1950

JOHN BOWACK *Antiquities of Middlesex*, S. Keble, 1705

MARY ELIZABETH BRADDON *The Rose of Life*, Hutchinson, 1905

FRANCES BURNEY *Evelina, or the History of a Young Lady's Entrance into the World*, 1778

R. CAMPBELL *The London Tradesman*, T. Gardner, 1747, reprinted David & Charles, 1969

JANE WELSH CARLYLE *A New Selection of her Letters*, arranged by Trudy Bliss, Gollancz, 1949

E. BERESFORD CHANCELLOR *The Eighteenth Century in London. An Account of its Social Life and Arts*, Batsford, 1920

E. BERESFORD CHANCELLOR *The West End of Yesterday and Today*, Architectural Press 1926

GEORGE CLINCH ed. *Soho and its Associations, Historical, Literary and Artistic*, from the MS of the late E. F. Rimbault, Dulau, 1895

KATHLEEN COBURN ed. *Sara Hutchinson, Letters 1800–35*, Routledge & Kegan Paul, 1954

REGINALD COLBY *Mayfair – A Town within London*, Country Life, 1966

ARTHUR COMPTON-RICKETT *The London Life of Yesterday*, Constable, 1909

THOMAS CREEVEY *Creevey's Life and Times. A further selection from the Correspondence of Thomas Creevey*, ed. John Gore, John Murray, 1891

PETER CUNNINGHAM *The Handbook of London*, John Murray, 1891

HENRY CURWEN *A History of Booksellers*, Chatto & Windus, 1873

ARTHUR I. DASENT *History of Grosvenor Square*, Macmillan, 1935

DOROTHY DAVIS *A History of Shopping*, Routledge & Kegan Paul, 1966

DANIEL DEFOE *The Complete English Tradesman*, 1726, reprinted with notes, William & Robert Chambers & W. S. Orr, 1839

ALAN DENT *My Covent Garden*, J. & M. Dent, 1973

CHARLES DICKENS *Sketches by Boz*, 1835–6

CHARLES DICKENS *Little Dorrit*, 1857

CHARLES DICKENS *Nicholas Nickleby*, published in monthly parts 1838–9

BRIAN DOBBS *The Last Shall be First – the Colourful Story of John Lobb the St. James's Bootmakers*, Elm Tree Books, Hamish Hamilton, 1972

LADY DUFF-GORDON (LUCILE) *Discretions and Indiscretions*, Frederick A. Stokes, New York, 1932

JOHN DUNTON *The Life and Errors of John Dunton, Citizen of London*, J. Nichols, Son & Bentley, 1818

J. J. DYOS and MICHAEL WOLFF *The Victorian City – Images and Realities*, Routledge & Kegan Paul, 1973

G. ELAND ed. *The Purefoy Letters, 1735–1753*, Sidgwick & Jackson, 1931

JOHN EVELYN *Diary, 1641–1706*, introduction and notes by Austin Dobson, Macmillan, 1908

THOMAS FAULKNER *History & Antiquities of Kensington*, printed by D. Jaques of Chelsea for T. Egerton, Whitehall, 1820

HENRY FIELDING *Tom Jones*, 1749

ROGER FULFORD *Votes for Women*, Faber & Faber, 1957

John Gay *Trivia, or the Art of Walking the Streets of London*, 1716

M. Dorothy George *London Life in the Eighteenth Century*, Kegan Paul, French, Trubner, 1925

Geoffrey A. Godden *Victorian Porcelain*, Herbert Jenkins, 1961

Catherine Grace Frances Gore *Women As They Are, or the Manners of the Day*, Henry Colburn & Richard Bentley, 1830

Catherine Grace Frances Gore *Mothers and Daughters*, Henry Colburn & Richard Bentley, 1831

Catherine Grace Frances Gore *Pin Money*, Henry Colburn & Richard Bentley, 1831

Rosamund Brunel Gotch *Mendelssohn and His Friends in Kensington – Letters from Fanny and Sophy Horsley, 1833–36*, Oxford University Press, 1934

Rees Howell Gronow *The Reminiscences and Recollections of Captain Gronow, 1810–60*, John C. Nimmo, 1892

George and Weedon Grossmith *The Diary of a Nobody, Punch* series 1888–9, 1st pub. book form 1892

Edward Hall ed. *Miss Weeton – Journal of a Governess, 1807–11*, Oxford University Press, 1936

Charles Harris *Islington*, Hamish Hamilton, 1974

Edward Hatton *A New View of London, or an Ample Account of that City*, 1708

A. L. Hayward ed. *The London Spy – The Vanities and Vices of the Town Exposed to View* by Edward Ward, Cassell, 1927

Ambrose Heal *London Tradesmen's Cards of the XVIII Century*, B. T. Batsford, 1925

Ambrose Heal *The Signboards of Old London Shops*, B. T. Batsford, 1947

John E. N. Hearsay *Young Mr Pepys*, Constable, 1973

Christopher Hibbert *London – The Biography of a City*, Longmans, 1969

Georgiana Hill *A History of English Dress*, Richard Bentley, 1893

Georgiana Hill *Women in English Life*, Richard Bentley, 1896

Hermione Hobhouse *The History of Regent Street*, Macdonald & Jane's in association with Queen Anne Press, 1975

Elizabeth Lady Holland *Letters to her Son, 1821–45*, ed. the Earl of Ilchester, John Murray, 1946

Thea Holme *Chelsea*, Hamish Hamilton, 1972

Derek Hudson *Munby, Man of Two Worlds. The Life and Diary of Arthur J. Munby, 1828–1910*, John Murray, 1972

M. Vivien Hughes *A London Family 1870–1900. A Trilogy*, Oxford University Press, 1946

Sara Hutchinson *Letters, 1800–35*, ed. Kathleen Coburn, Routledge & Kegan Paul, 1954

James B. Jefferys *Retail Trading in Great Britain, 1850–1950*, Cambridge University Press, 1954

Charles Letheridge Kingsford *The Early History of Piccadilly, Leicester Square, Soho, and their Neighbourhoods*, based on a plan drawn in 1585 and published by the London Topographical Society in 1925, Cambridge University Press, 1925

Charles Knight ed. *London*, Vol. V. 1843, reprinted Henry G. Bohn, 1851

Charles Knight *Shadows of the Old Booksellers*, 1865, reprinted Peter Davies, 1927

James Lackington *Memoirs of the first 45 years of the Life of James Lackington*, printed for the author at No. 46 & 47 Chiswell Street, 1792

Charles and Mary Anne Lamb *Letters*, Vol. II, 1801–9, ed. Edwin W. Marrs, Jr, Cornell University Press, Ithaca & London, 1976

Richard Lambert *The Universal Provider, A Study of William Whiteley and the Rise of the London Department Store*, Harrap, 1938

Osbert Lancaster *All Done from Memory*, John Murray, 1953

Lord William Pitt Lennox *Fashion Then and Now*, Chapman & Hall, 1878

Edward Bulwer Lytton *Pelham, or Adventures of a Gentleman*, 1828

W. Maitland *A History and Survey of London*, edition of 1756

James Peller Malcolm *Anecdotes of the Manners and Customs of London during the Eighteenth Century*, Longman, Hurst, Rees, and Orme, 1810

Dorothy Marshall *Eighteenth Century England*, Longmans, 1962

Dorothy Marshall *Dr. Johnson's London*, John Wiley, New York, 1968

HENRY MAYHEW *London Labour and the London Poor, 1851*, ed. Peter Quennell, Spring Books, 1969

HENRY MAYHEW ed. *The Shops and Companies of London, and the Trades and Manufactories of Great Britain,* Strand Printing and Publishing Co., 1865

CECIL A. MEADOWS *Trade Signs and their Origins,* Routledge & Kegan Paul, 1957

NANCY MITFORD ed. *The Ladies of Alderley. The letters between Maria Josepha, Lady Stanley of Alderley and her daughter-in-law, 1841–50,* Chapman & Hall, 1938

DORIS LANGLEY MOORE *Lord Byron – Accounts Rendered,* John Murray, 1974

STANLEY MORISON *John Bell, 1745–1831,* Cambridge University Press, 1930

D. W. PEEL *A Garden in the Sky. The Story of Barkers of Kensington, 1870–1957,* W. H. Allen, 1960

CHARLES PENDRILL *Old Parish Life in London,* Oxford University Press, 1937

SAMUEL PEPYS *Diary,* edition of 1923, ed. Henry B. Wheatley, Oxford University Press, 1937

VALERIE PIRIE *A Frenchman Sees the English in the 'Fifties. Adapted from the French of Francis Wey,* Sidgwick & Jackson, 1935

FRANK PODMORE *Robert Owen – A Biography,* Hutchinson, 1906

JAMES POPE-HENNESSY *Queen Mary, 1867–1953,* Allen & Unwin, 1959

UNA POPE-HENNESSY *Charles Dickens,* Chatto & Windus, 1945

REGINALD POUND *Selfridge – A Biography,* Heinemann, 1960

The Purefoy Letters, 1735–1753, ed. G. Eland, Sidgwick & Jackson, 1931

REV. J. RICHARDSON *Recollections of the Last Half Century,* Saville & Edwards, 1855

E. F. RIMBAULT *Soho and its Associations, Historical, Literary and Artistic,* ed. George Clinch, Dulau of Soho Square, 1895

SOPHIE VON LA ROCHE *Sophie in London, 1786,* transl. from the German by Clare Williams, Jonathan Cape, 1933

GEORGE AUGUSTUS SALA *Twice Round the Clock, or the Hours of the Day and Night in London,* Houlston & Wright, 1859

ANN L. SAUNDERS *Regent's Park. A Study of the Development of the Area from 1086 to the Present Day,* David & Charles, 1969

G. SCOTT THOMPSON *The Russells in Bloomsbury, 1669–1771,* Jonathan Cape, 1940

FRANCIS SHEPPARD *London 1808–1870: The Infernal Wen,* Secker & Warburg, 1971

GEORGE SMITH and FRANK BENGER *The Oldest London Bookshop, 1728–1928,* Ellis, 1928

J. T. SMITH *Nollekens and His Times,* 1828, reprinted Turnstile Press, 1949

ROBERT SOUTHEY *Letters from England by Don Manuel Alvarez Espriella,* Longmans, 1807

JOHN STOW *Survey of London; Brought down to the Present by J. Strype,* 1720

RALPH STRAUSS *Sala – The Portrait of an Eminent Victorian,* Constable, 1942

JOHN SUMMERSON *Georgian London,* Pleiades Books, 1945

W. M. THACKERAY *Vanity Fair,* 1847

W. M. THACKERAY *The History of Pendennis,* 1848

HUGH TOURS *The Life and Letters of Emma Hamilton,* Gollancz, 1963

CHRISTOPHER TRENT *The Russells,* Frederick Muller, 1966

HORACE WALPOLE *Letters, 1732–1797*

EDWARD WARD *The London Spy – The Vanities and Vices of the Town Exposed to View,* in monthly parts from 1698, volume form 1703, ed. A. L. Hayward, Cassell, 1927

MISS WEETON *Journal of a Governess, 1807–1811,* ed. Edward Hall, Oxford University Press, 1936

CHARLES WELSH *A Bookseller of the Last Century. Being some Account of the Life of John Newbery,* Griffith, Farren, Okeden & Welsh, 1885

FRANCIS WEY *A Frenchman Sees the English in the 'Fifties,* adapted by Valerie Pirie from *Les Anglais chez Eux,* Sidgwick & Jackson, 1935

H. B. WHEATLEY *Bond Street Old and New, 1686–1911,* Fine Art Society, 1911

H. B. WHEATLEY *London Past and Present. Its History, Associations and Traditions,* based on *The Handbook of London* by the late Peter Cunningham, John Murray, 1891

W. B. WHITAKER *Victorian and Edwardian Shopworkers – The Struggle to obtain better conditions and a half-holiday,* David & Charles, 1973

FRANK WHITBOURN *Mr. Lock of St. James's Street*, Heinemann, 1971

NATHANIEL WHITTOCK *The Complete Book of Trades*, J. Bennet, 1837

A. H. WILLIAMS *No Name on the Door – a Memoir of Gordon Selfridge*, W. H. Allen, 1956

CLARE WILLIAMS ed. and transl. from German *Sophie in London, 1786*, Jonathan Cape, 1933

FREDERICK WILLIS *A Book of London Yesterdays*, Phoenix House, 1960

HARRIETTE WILSON *Memoirs of Herself and Others*, Stockdale, 1825, reprinted Peter Davis, 1929

G. M. YOUNG ed. *Early Victorian England, 1830–1865*, Vol. I, Section III, *Town Life* by R. H. Mottram, Oxford University Press, 1934

Privately printed books

The Fenwick Story by Reginald Pound, 1972

Thomas Goode of London, 1827–1977 by Philip M. Rayner

Harrods – A Story of British Achievement, 1849–1949

Sir Ambrose Heal – A Booklet to Commemorate the Centenary Exhibition of his Life and Work, 1872–1959

Lillywhite's 1863–1963 – A Century in the Service of Sport by Alison Adburgham

A Short History of Kensington Square by H. Avray Tipping, 1942

The House of Maple – Private Enterprise, a Century of Service, 1941

Old Marylebone and Some of its Famous People by H. J. Matthews, n.d.

Tribute to Nash – Architect and Planner (catalogue of exhibition at Austin Reed on the occasion of the 150th anniversary of Regent Street), 1975

The Story of W. H. Smith & Sons by G. R. Pockleton, 1921

Guide Books and Trade Directories

Grand Architectural Panorama of London, I. Whitelaw, 1849

Johnston's Commercial Guide & Trade Directory, 1817

Modern London – The World's Metropolis, The Historical Publishing Co., 1887

The Picture of London. Being a Correct Guide to all the Curiosities, Amusements, Exhibitions, Public Establishments, and Remarkable Objects in and near London,

Richard Phillips, editions from 1802 to 1807

Survey of London, Vols. XX, XXI, XXIX, XXX, XXXI, XXXII, XXXIX. General editor F. H. W. Sheppard, Athlone Press, University of London

Tallis's Street Views – A Complete Stranger's Guide through London, editions from 1838 to 1840

A Visit to Regent Street, London, printed by Henry Vizetelly, c. 1860

Periodicals

Ackermann's Repository of the Arts, Literature, Fashion, Manufactures, etc., 1824–28

Ainsworth's Magazine, 1843

Architectural Review: 'A Century of Regent Street', December 1927; 'Give the customers what they want', May 1977

Chamber's Journal of Popular Literature, Science and Art, Fourth Series, 15 October 1869, 'The London Shop Fronts'

Country Life: 'Six Centuries of a London Market' (Leadenhall) by Nicholas Roskill, 23 January 1958; 'Europe's First Department Store' by G. Bernard Hughes, 15 May 1958; 'The Building of Belgravia' by H. Hobhouse, 8 May 1969

The Drapers' Record, from 1887

Economic History Review, Second Series, Vol. XII, 1959–60, 'Josiah Wedgwood: an Eighteenth Century Entrepreneur in Salesmanship and Marketing Techniques', by N. McKendrick

The Female Tatler by Mrs Crackenthorpe (Mrs Mary de la Rivière Manley), 1709–10

Fortnightly Review, 'The Ethics of Shopping' by Lady Jeune, January 1895

The Gazette of the John Lewis Partnership

Gentleman's Magazine, Betty Neale's obituary, May 1797

Illustrated London News: Lewis & Allenby, 14 April 1866; Regent Street in the Season, 21 April 1866

The Liberty Lamp, staff magazine of Liberty & Co.

Punch, from 1841

Westminster Review, review of *Pin Money*, October 1831

The World of Fashion, 1824–51

Illustration acknowledgments

Half-title: Trade card of Mary and Ann Hogarth. Attributed to William Hogarth.

Title-page: Swan and Edgar's department store, Piccadilly Circus, 1910. Photo National Monuments Record.

6 Detail from *Crooked Lane*. Watercolour by George Scharf, c. 1840. Guildhall Library, City of London.

8 Shops at Bishopsgate, 1736. Engraving after R. West. Greater London Council Print Collection.

9 *The Compleat Auctioner*. Engraving by Sutton Nicholl, c. 1700. Guildhall Library, City of London.

10 Portrait of Samuel Pepys. Painting after Peter Lely, c. 1670. The Master and Fellows of Magdalene College, Cambridge.

11 *top*. Plan of the City and environs of London, 1642–43. British Museum, London.

11 *bottom*. View of London in the 17th century. Engraving by Visscher. Museum of London.

14 Somerset House from the river. Engraving by J. Kip after L. Knyff, 1707.

15 The Royal Exchange. Engraving by Franciscus Hogenberg, 1569. British Museum, London.

17 Interior of Westminster Hall. Engraving after Gravelot, 1797. Guildhall Library, City of London.

19 Old Leadenhall Market in the 19th century. Engraving after J. Sulman. Guildhall Library, City of London.

22–3 *left*. Old houses at the west corner of Chancery Lane. Etching by J. T. Smith, 1781. British Museum, London.

22–3 *top*. Old London Bridge. Painting by Claude de Jongh, c. 1639. Greater London Council as Trustees of the Iveagh Bequest, Kenwood. Photo Greater London Council.

22–3 *bottom*. Cheapside in 1638. Anonymous engraving. Guildhall Library, City of London.

24 Trade card of John Richardson, grocer, 1756.

25 *top*. Covent Garden piazza. Etching by W. Hollar, c. 1640. British Museum, London.

25 *bottom*. Bloomsbury Square in the 18th century. Engraving by Sutton Nicholl, Museum of London.

26 Pell-mell player. British Museum, London.

27 Details of a pickadill. From *A Handbook of English Costume in the 17th Century*, Faber & Faber, 1955.

29 *right*. The May fair in progress, c. 1716. Museum of London.

29 *left*. A coffee house in the early 18th century. From *Vulgus Britannicus*, 1710.

30 Interior of Berry Brothers' premises, St James's Street. Courtesy Berry Bros. & Rudd.

31 *left*. A page recording the weight of Beau Brummell. Courtesy Berry Bros. & Rudd.

31 *right*. The Great Scales at Berry Brothers. Painting by Frank Dadd, 1911. Courtesy Berry Bros. & Rudd.

33 Fortnum & Mason, Piccadilly, in 1837. Courtesy Fortnum & Mason.

34 St James's Street. From G. W. Thornbury, *Old and New London*, 1873.

35 *top*. Lock's hat shop in St James's Street. Courtesy James Lock and Co. Ltd.

35 *bottom*. Lock's hat label. Courtesy James Lock and Co. Ltd.

36–7 *top*. Cheapside and St Mary-le-Bow. Engraving by T. Bowles, 1751. Guildhall Library, City of London.

36–7 *bottom*. Trade card of John Flude. 18th century. Museum of London.

36–7 *left*. Trade card of Benjamin Cole, 1710–20. Museum of London.

38 Trade card of John Snowdon, 1764. Museum of London.

39 *The City 'Prentice at his Master's Door*. Engraving by William Hogarth. British Museum, London.

41 *The Tailor's Shop*. Pen and ink by L. P. Boitard, before 1749. Royal Library, Windsor Castle. Reproduced by gracious permission of Her Majesty the Queen.

42 Stay-maker's shop, late 17th century. Mansell Collection.

43 *A Milliner's Shop*, 1789. Mansell Collection.

45 *left*. Monmouth Street. Sketch by George Cruikshank.

45 *right*. *Old Cloaks Suits or Coats*. Engraving by P. Tempest after M. Lauron, early 18th century. Museum of London.

46 Signboard of the Three Pigeons, c. 1750.

47 *The Unlucky Glance*. Engraving attributed to Gravelot, from *Town and Country Magazine*, 1772.

48 Interior of Lackington and Allen, Temple of the Muses, Finsbury Square. From *The Repository of Arts*, April 1809. Guildhall Library, City of London.

49 *left*. Trade card of Francis Noble's Circulating Library.

49 *right*. Frontage of Hatchard's Bookshop, Piccadilly. Courtesy Hatchard's.

50–1 *top left*. The Strand and St Mary's Church. Engraving by T. Malton, 1796. Guildhall Library, City of London.

50–1 *top right*. R. Ackermann's print shop in the Strand. Coloured engraving. Guildhall Library, City of London.

50–1 *bottom left*. Hungerford Market. Engraving after Thomas Shepherd, early 19th century. Greater London Council Print Collection.

50–1 *bottom right*. Opening Day at the New Hungerford Market, 2 July 1833. Engraving after R. W. Billings. Guildhall Library, City of London.

53 Interior of Ackermann's print shop. After Pugin and Rowlandson, 1809. Guildhall Library, City of London.

54 Title-page of *La Belle Assemblée*, vol. II, 1807.

55 South-east view of Kensington and St Mary Abbott's. After an engraving by J. Chatelain, *c.* 1750. Museum of London.

56 Hyde Park Corner. Engraving, *c.* 1750. Radio Times Hulton Picture Library.

57 *North Country Mails at the Peacock*, 1821. Oil painting by James Pollard. Collection of Mr and Mrs Paul Mellon.

58 Figure of a Highlander. 18th-century tobacconists' sign. Museum of London.

59 Chippendale design for a state bed. From *The Gentleman and Cabinet Maker's Directory*, 1762.

61 *left.* Trade card of William Conaway, lamplighter, showing Monmouth House, Soho Square.

61 *right.* The sign of the Bleeder, signboard of Samuel Darkin, surgeon, *c.* 1720.

2–3 *top left.* Wedgwood medallions depicting Sir William Hamilton (top), George III (left) and Admiral Keppel (right). Victoria and Albert Museum, London.

2–3 *bottom left.* Trade card of Charles Blyde.

2–3 *right.* Wedgwood and Byerley showrooms at York Street, St James's Square. From *The Repository of Arts*, 1809.

65 *Summer Amusement.* 18th-century print. Greater London Council Print Collection.

66 *top.* Tyburn turnpike, *c.* 1792. After Rowlandson. Museum of London.

66 *bottom.* The Pantheon, Oxford Street, in the early 19th century. From an engraving after Thomas Shepherd, *c.* 1828.

67 *top.* Marylebone Road in 1793. Wash drawing by S. H. Grimm. British Library, London, Mss 15542.

67 *bottom.* Detail of Fairburn's map of London and Westminster, 1801. Museum of London.

68 Trade card of Clark and Debenham, Wigmore Street, 1813.

69 Trade card of William Guest, 18th century. Museum of London.

70 The dairy in Golden Lane. Drawing after G. Scharf, 1835. Greater London Council Print Collection.

71 Oxford Market, late 19th century. Guildhall Library, City of London.

73 *left.* Lamplighters. After an engraving by W. H. Pyne, 1808. Museum of London.

73 *right.* *A Peep at the gaslight in Pall Mall.* Cartoon by Thomas Rowlandson, 1809. The Science Museum, London.

74 Trade card of John Brindley.

75 Trade card of Jane Taylor and Son.

76 *The Dandy Club.* Drawing by Richard Dighton, 1818. British Museum, London.

77 *left.* George ('Beau') Brummell. Engraving after John Cooke. British Museum, London.

77 *right.* Bulwer Lytton, 1832. From *Fraser's Magazine*.

79 Late 18th-century shopfront of Fribourg & Treyer, Haymarket. National Monuments Record.

80 Schomberg House. Watercolour by Thomas Shepherd, *c.* 1850. Greater London Council Print Collection.

81 Interior of Harding, Howell & Co., Pall Mall. From *The Repository of Arts*, 1809.

83 Chintz samples from *The Repository of Arts*, February 1811.

85 *far left.* Fashions in 1830. From *La Belle Assemblée*, October 1830.

85 *right.* Title-page of *The World of Fashion*, vol. XIII, 1836. Chelsea Public Library. Photo Eileen Tweedy.

86 Portrait of Samuel Birch, Lord Mayor in 1815. After a painting by S. Drummond. Guildhall Library, City of London.

87 *above.* Carrier's waggon. Detail from *The Mansion House from the Bank*. Engraving after Thomas Shepherd, 19th century. Greater London Council Print Collection.

87 *below.* Cheapside, looking west. Engraving after Thomas Shepherd, 1831. British Museum, London.

88 *The Duke of Beaufort Coach leaving the Bull and Mouth, Piccadilly.* Engraving by C. Hunt after a painting by W. G. Shayer, 1841. Guildhall Library, City of London.

91 *top.* Publication of the '*Times' Newspaper: outside the office.* From a drawing by William McConnell in Augustus Sala, *Twice Round the Clock*, 1859.

91 *bottom.* W. H. Smith bookstall at King's Cross Station, end of 19th century. Courtesy W. H. Smith.

93 *left.* Bonnets, 1817. From *The Repository of Arts*, 1817.

93 *right.* *The Haberdasher Dandy.* Cartoon by C. Williams, early 19th century. Guildhall Library, City of London.

95 Sir Robert Waithman, Lord Mayor in 1824, by Richard Dighton, 1821. Guildhall Library, City of London.

97 'A Street Courtship' from W. M. Thackeray, *The Christmas Books of Mr. M. A. Titmarsh*, 1868.

98 Plan showing Regent Street as laid out by John Nash, 1812–27.

99 *top.* Regent Street, the Quadrant. Engraving after Thomas Shepherd, 1827, from James Elmes, *Metropolitan Improvements*, 1827.

99 *bottom.* Verrey's restaurant, Regent Street, 1910. Photo National Monuments Record.

101 St James's Market, *c.* 1840. Greater London Council Print Collection.

102 Interior of Burlington Arcade. 19th-

century engraving.

103 Burlington Arcade. 19th-century engraving after Thomas Shepherd. Guildhall Library, City of London.

104–5 Exeter Change, the Strand. 19th-century engraving by George Cooke. Guildhall Library, City of London.

105 Lowther Arcade, the Strand. From Felix Leigh, *London Town*, 1833.

107 *left.* Premises of Heal & Son Ltd, Tottenham Court Road. National Monuments Record.

107 *right.* Design for a bed, from Heal's catalogue of 1852. Courtesy Heal & Son Ltd. Photo Eileen Tweedy.

108 Advertisement of J. & J. Holmes.

109 *Scene in Belgrave Square.* Watercolour by Eugene Lami, *c.* 1850. Victoria and Albert Museum, London.

110 East side of Belgrave Square. Engraving after G. B. Moore, 1828.

111 Advertisement of Farmer & Rogers, 1866. Mansell Collection.

113 Fortnum & Mason bill, 1816. Courtesy Fortnum & Mason.

116 *left.* View of Regent Street. Engraving after R. Sandeman, from *The Grand Architectural Panorama of London*, 1849.

116 *right.* Interior of Howell, James & Co, Regent Street, 1859. Mansell Collection.

117 *Berkeley Square 5 p.m.* Drawing and verses from *Punch*, 24 August 1867.

118–9 *top left.* Removal of the Quadrant colonnades in 1848. B. T. Batsford.

118–9 *bottom left.* Regent Street. From the *Illustrated London News*, March 1849.

118–9 *top right.* The Quadrant, Regent Street, in 1852. Greater London Council Print Collection.

118–9 *bottom right.* Peter Robinson, Oxford Street, 1910. National Monuments Record.

120 Scott Adie advertisement for a 'Tartan Maud'.

121 *top.* Advertisement of Jay's General Mourning Warehouse, 1888. Mansell Collection.

121 *bottom.* Jay's General Mourning Warehouse, Regent Street, in the mid 19th century. From *A Visit to Regent Street.*

122 Nicholson's of St Paul's Churchyard.

123 Nicholson's bill, 1888.

124 View of Regent Street. Engraving after R. Sandeman, from *The Grand Architectural Panorama of London*, 1849.

125 Trade card of Scott Adie. 19th century. Courtesy Scott Adie.

126 'The Resilient Boot', sold by Medwin & Co. Ltd. From *A Visit to Regent Street.*

127 *left.* 'Travelling Portmanteau', sold by H. J. & D. Nicoll. From *A Visit to Regent Street.*

127 *right.* Interior of H. J. & D. Nicoll, mid 19th century. From *A Visit to Regent Street.*

129 *Eight o'clock a.m.: opening shop.* From a drawing by William McConnell in Augustus Sala, *Twice Round the Clock*, 1859.

130 Portrait of Mr Peter Jones. Courtesy John Lewis Partnership.

131 Early view of Kensington High Street in 1865. National Monuments Record.

132 Harrod's shop in Brompton Road, 1892. National Monuments Record.

133 The Chelsea Bunn House. Engraving attributed to William Hogarth, *c.* 1730.

136–7 *top left.* Peter Jones' department store, Sloane Square, early 20th century. Courtesy John Lewis Partnership.

136–7 *bottom left.* John Lewis' premises, Oxford Street in the 1880s. Courtesy John Lewis Partnership.

136–7 *right.* Interior of Peter Jones' store in 1890. Courtesy John Lewis Partnership.

138 'Special Smoking Mixture'. From the Army & Navy Stores catalogue, 1913.

139 Peter Robinson's premises, 1891. Mansell Collection.

140 Advertisement of W. Gillingwater, Upper Street, Islington, 1848. Islington Public Libraries. Photo Jim Connell.

141 Westbourne Grove in 1884. Greater London Council Photographic Library.

143 *left.* John Barker's department store, Kensington High Street, in the late 19th century. From *Modern London.*

143 *right.* Sir John Barker. From *Vanity Fair* magazine. Kensington and Chelsea Public Libraries.

145 Interior of Ponting's, Kensington High Street, 1913. National Monuments Record.

147 *The Free Englishman* by Jack Dodsworth, late 19th century. Union of Shop, Distributive and Allied Workers.

148 Hair-restorer, ear-trumpet and dinner gong, from the Army & Navy Stores catalogue, 1907.

149 *top.* Advertisement for a sale at the Bon Marché on a Brixton tram, 1894. Courtesy John Lewis Partnership.

149 *bottom.* The Bon Marché department store, Brixton, in the 1960s. Courtesy John Lewis Partnership.

151 *left.* Sir Arthur Lasenby Liberty. Painting by Arthur Hacker, 1913. Photo Eileen Tweedy.

151 *right.* Mr John Lewis at his Hampstead home on 24 February 1927. Courtesy John Lewis Partnership.

152–3 *left.* An ABC teashop. Sketch by H. Thomson, from E. T. Cook *Highways and Byways of London*, Macmillan and Co. Ltd, 1902.

152–3 *right.* Piccadilly in the 1880s.

154 From Liberty's catalogue *Silks, c.* 1896. Courtesy Liberty and Co. Ltd.

155 *top.* Marshall and Snelgrove's department store, Oxford Street, late 19th century. Mansell Collection.

155 *bottom. Happy Thought. Punch,* 2 June 1877.

Index

Figures in italics at the end of entries refer to page numbers of illustrations